Testimonials for

Introduction to Logic Programming

This is a book for the 21st century: presenting an elegant and innovative perspective on logic programming. Unlike other texts, it takes datasets as a fundamental notion, thereby bridging the gap between programming languages and knowledge representation languages; and it treats updates on an equal footing with datasets, leading to a sound and practical treatment of action and change.

Bob Kowalski, Professor Emeritus, Imperial College London

In a world where Deep Learning and Python are the talk of the day, this book is a remarkable development. It introduces the reader to the fundamentals of traditional Logic Programming and makes clear the benefits of using the technology to create runnable specifications for complex systems.

Son Cao Tran, Professor in Computer Science, New Mexico State University

Excellent introduction to the fundamentals of Logic Programming. The book is well-written and well-structured. Concepts are explained clearly and the gradually increasing complexity of exercises makes it so that one can understand easy notions quickly before moving on to more difficult ideas.

George Younger, student, Stanford University

Introduction to Logic Programming

Synthesis Lectures on Artificial Intelligence and Machine Learning

Introduction to Logic Programming
Michael Genesereth and Vinay K. Chaudhri
2020

Federated Learning
Qiang Yang, Yang Liu, Yong Cheng, Yan Kang, Tianjian Chen, and Han Yu
2019

An Introduction to the Planning Domain Definition Language
Patrik Haslum, Nir Lipovetzky, Daniele Magazzeni, and Christian Muise
2019

Reasoning with Probabilistic and Deterministic Graphical Models: Exact Algorithms, Second Edition
Rina Dechter
2019

Learning and Decision-Making from Rank Data
Lirong Xia
2019

Lifelong Machine Learning, Second Edition
Zhiyuan Chen and Bing Liu
2018

Adversarial Machine Learning
Yevgeniy Vorobeychik and Murat Kantarcioglu
2018

Strategic Voting
Reshef Meir
2018

Predicting Human Decision-Making: From Prediction to Action
Ariel Rosenfeld and Sarit Kraus
2018

Game Theory for Data Science: Eliciting Truthful Information
Boi Faltings and Goran Radanovic
2017

Multi-Objective Decision Making
Diederik M. Roijers and Shimon Whiteson
2017

Lifelong Machine Learning
Zhiyuan Chen and Bing Liu
2016

Statistical Relational Artificial Intelligence: Logic, Probability, and Computation
Luc De Raedt, Kristian Kersting, Sriraam Natarajan, and David Poole
2016

Representing and Reasoning with Qualitative Preferences: Tools and Applications
Ganesh Ram Santhanam, Samik Basu, and Vasant Honavar
2016

Metric Learning
Aurélien Bellet, Amaury Habrard, and Marc Sebban
2015

Graph-Based Semi-Supervised Learning
Amarnag Subramanya and Partha Pratim Talukdar
2014

Robot Learning from Human Teachers
Sonia Chernova and Andrea L. Thomaz
2014

General Game Playing
Michael Genesereth and Michael Thielscher
2014

Judgment Aggregation: A Primer
Davide Grossi and Gabriella Pigozzi
2014

An Introduction to Constraint-Based Temporal Reasoning
Roman Barták, Robert A. Morris, and K. Brent Venable
2014

Reasoning with Probabilistic and Deterministic Graphical Models: Exact Algorithms
Rina Dechter
2013

Introduction to Intelligent Systems in Traffic and Transportation
Ana L.C. Bazzan and Franziska Klügl
2013

A Concise Introduction to Models and Methods for Automated Planning
Hector Geffner and Blai Bonet
2013

Essential Principles for Autonomous Robotics
Henry Hexmoor
2013

Case-Based Reasoning: A Concise Introduction
Beatriz López
2013

Answer Set Solving in Practice
Martin Gebser, Roland Kaminski, Benjamin Kaufmann, and Torsten Schaub
2012

Planning with Markov Decision Processes: An AI Perspective
Mausam and Andrey Kolobov
2012

Active Learning
Burr Settles
2012

Computational Aspects of Cooperative Game Theory
Georgios Chalkiadakis, Edith Elkind, and Michael Wooldridge
2011

Representations and Techniques for 3D Object Recognition and Scene Interpretation
Derek Hoiem and Silvio Savarese
2011

A Short Introduction to Preferences: Between Artificial Intelligence and Social Choice
Francesca Rossi, Kristen Brent Venable, and Toby Walsh
2011

Human Computation
Edith Law and Luis von Ahn
2011

Trading Agents
Michael P. Wellman
2011

Visual Object Recognition
Kristen Grauman and Bastian Leibe
2011

Learning with Support Vector Machines
Colin Campbell and Yiming Ying
2011

Algorithms for Reinforcement Learning
Csaba Szepesvári
2010

Data Integration: The Relational Logic Approach
Michael Genesereth
2010

Markov Logic: An Interface Layer for Artificial Intelligence
Pedro Domingos and Daniel Lowd
2009

Introduction to Semi-Supervised Learning
XiaojinZhu and Andrew B.Goldberg
2009

Action Programming Languages
Michael Thielscher
2008

Representation Discovery using Harmonic Analysis
Sridhar Mahadevan
2008

Essentials of Game Theory: A Concise Multidisciplinary Introduction
Kevin Leyton-Brown and Yoav Shoham
2008

A Concise Introduction to Multiagent Systems and Distributed Artificial Intelligence
Nikos Vlassis
2007

Intelligent Autonomous Robotics: A Robot Soccer Case Study
Peter Stone
2007

Introduction to Logic Programming

Michael Genesereth and Vinay K. Chaudhri

www.morganclaypool.com

ISBN: 9781681737225 paperback
ISBN: 9781681737232 ebook
ISBN: 9781681737249 hardcover

DOI 10.2200/S00966ED1V01Y201911AIM044

A Publication in the Morgan & Claypool Publishers series
SYNTHESIS LECTURES ON ARTIFICIAL INTELLIGENCE AND MACHINE LEARNING

Lecture #44
Series Editors: Ronald Brachman, *Jacobs Technion-Cornell Institute at Cornell Tech*
Francesca Rossi, *IBM Research AI*
Peter Stone, *University of Texas at Austin*

Series ISSN
Synthesis Lectures on Artificial Intelligence and Machine Learning
Print 1939-4608 Electronic 1939-4616

Introduction to Logic Programming

Michael Genesereth and Vinay K. Chaudhri
Stanford University

SYNTHESIS LECTURES ON ARTIFICIAL INTELLIGENCE AND MACHINE LEARNING #44

MORGAN & CLAYPOOL PUBLISHERS

ABSTRACT

Logic Programming is a style of programming in which programs take the form of sets of sentences in the language of Symbolic Logic. Over the years, there has been growing interest in Logic Programming due to applications in deductive databases, automated worksheets, Enterprise Management (business rules), Computational Law, and General Game Playing. This book introduces Logic Programming theory, current technology, and popular applications.

In this volume, we take an innovative, model-theoretic approach to logic programming. We begin with the fundamental notion of datasets, i.e., sets of ground atoms. Given this fundamental notion, we introduce views, i.e., virtual relations; and we define classical logic programs as sets of view definitions, written using traditional Prolog-like notation but with semantics given in terms of datasets rather than implementation. We then introduce actions, i.e., additions and deletions of ground atoms; and we define dynamic logic programs as sets of action definitions.

In addition to the printed book, there is an online version of the text with an interpreter and a compiler for the language used in the text and an integrated development environment for use in developing and deploying practical logic programs.

KEYWORDS

logic programming, computational logic, knowledge representation, deductive databases, aritificial intelligence

Contents

Preface

This book is an introductory textbook on Logic Programming. It is intended primarily for use at the undergraduate level. However, it can be used for motivated secondary school students, and it can be used at the start of graduate school for those who have not yet seen the material.

There are just two prerequisites. The book presumes that the student understands sets and set operations, such as union, intersection, and so forth. The book also presumes that the student is comfortable with symbolic mathematics, at the level of high-school algebra or beyond. Nothing else is required.

While experience in computational thinking is helpful, it is not essential. And prior programming experience is not necessary. In fact, we have observed that some students with programming backgrounds have *more* difficulty at first than students who are not accomplished programmers! It is almost as if they need to unlearn some things in order to appreciate the power and beauty of Logic Programming.

The approach to Logic Programming taken here emerged from more than 30 years of research, applications, and teaching of this material in both academic and commercial settings. The result of this experience is an approach to the subject matter that differs somewhat from the approach taken in other books on the subject in two essential ways.

First of all, in this volume, we take a model-theoretic approach to specifying semantics rather than the traditional proof-theoretic approach. We begin with the fundamental notion of *datasets*, i.e., sets of ground atoms. Given this fundamental notion, we introduce classic logic programs as *view definitions*, written using traditional Prolog notation but with semantics given in terms of datasets rather than implementation. (We also talk about implementation, but it comes later in the presentation.)

Another difference from other books on Logic Programming is that we treat change on an equal footing with state. Having talked about datasets, we introduce the fundamental notion of *updates*, i.e., additions and deletions of ground atoms. Given this fundamental notion, we introduce dynamic logic programs as sets of *action definitions*, where actions are conceptualized as sets of simultaneous updates. This extension allows us to talk about *logical agents* as well as static *logic programs*. (A logical agent is effectively a state machine in which each state is modeled as a dataset and each arc is modeled as a set of updates.)

In addition to the text of the book in print and online, there is a website with automatically graded online exercises, programming assignments, Logic Programming tools, and a variety of sample applications. The website (`http://logicprogramming.stanford.edu`) is free to use and open to all.

In conclusion, we first of all want to acknowledge the influence of two individuals who had a profound effect on our work here - Jeff Ullman and Bob Kowalski. Jeff Ullman, our colleague at Stanford, inspired us with his popular textbooks and helped us to appreciate the deep relationship between Logic Programming and databases. Bob Kowalski, co-inventor of Logic Programming, listened to our ideas, nurtured our work, and even collaborated on some of the material presented here.

We also want to acknowledge the contributions of a former graduate student - Abhijeet Mohapatra. He is a co-inventor of dynamic logic programming and the co-creator of many of the programming tools associated with our approach to Logic Programming. He helped to teach the course, worked with students, and offered invaluable suggestions on the presentation and organization of the material.

Finally, our thanks to the students who have had to endure early versions of this material, in many cases helping to get it right by suffering through experiments that were not always successful. It is a testament to the intelligence of these students that they seem to have learned the material despite multiple mistakes on our part. Their patience and constructive comments were invaluable in helping us to understand what works and what does not.

Michael Genesereth and Vinay K. Chaudhri
December 2019

PART I

Introduction

CHAPTER 1
Introduction

1.1 PROGRAMMING IN LOGIC

Logic Programming is a style of programming in which programs take the form of sets of sentences in the language of Symbolic Logic. Programs written in this style are called *logic programs*. The language in which these programs are written is called *logic programming language*. And a computer system that manages the creation and execution of logic programs is called a *logic programming system*.

1.2 LOGIC PROGRAMS AS RUNNABLE SPECIFICATIONS

Logic Programming is often said to be *declarative* or *descriptive* and contrasts with the *imperative* or *prescriptive* approach to programming associated with traditional programming languages.

In imperative/prescriptive programming, the programmer provides a detailed operational program for a system in terms of internal processing details (such as data types and variable assignments). In writing such programs, programmers typically take into account information about the intended application areas and goals of their programs, but that information is rarely recorded in the resulting programs, except in the form of non-executable comments.

In declarative/descriptive programming, programmers explicitly encode information about the application area and the goals of the program, but they do not specify internal processing details, leaving it to the systems that execute those programs to decide on those details on their own.

As an intuitive example of this distinction, consider the task of programming a robot to navigate from one point in a building to a second point. A typical imperative program would direct the robot to move forward a certain amount (or until its sensors indicated a suitable landmark); it would then tell the robot to turn and move forward again; and so forth until the robot arrives at the destination. By contrast, a typical declarative program would consist of a map and an indication of the starting and ending points on the map and would leave it to the robot to decide how to proceed.

A logic program is a type of declarative program in that it describes the application area of the program and the goals the programmer would like to achieve. It focusses on *what* is true and *what* is wanted rather than *how* to achieve the desired goals. In this respect, a logic program is more of a *specification* than an *implementation*.

Logic Programming is practical because there are well-known mechanical techniques for executing logic programs and/or producing traditional programs that achieve the same results. For this reason, logic programs are sometimes called *runnable specifications*.

1.3 ADVANTAGES OF LOGIC PROGRAMMING

Logic programs are typically *easier to create* and *easier to modify* than traditional programs. Programmers can get by with little or no knowledge of the capabilities and limitations of the systems executing those programs, and they do not need to choose specific methods of achieving their programs' goals.

Logic programs are *more composable* than traditional programs. In writing logic programs, programmers do not need to make arbitrary choices. As a result, logic programs can be combined with each other more easily than traditional programs where unnecessary arbitrary choices can conflict.

Logic programs are also more *agile* than traditional programs. A system executing a logic program can readily adapt to unexpected changes to its assumptions and/or its goals. Once again consider the robot described in the preceding section. If a robot running a logic program learns that a corridor is unexpectedly closed, it can choose a different corridor. If the robot is asked to pick up and deliver some goods along the way, it can combine routes to accomplish both tasks without having to accomplish them individually.

Finally, logic programs are more *versatile* than traditional programs—they can be used for multiple purposes, often without modification. Suppose we have a table of parents and children. Now, imagine that we are given definitions for standard kinship relations. For example, we are told that a grandparent is the parent of a parent. That single definition can be used as the basis for multiple traditional programs. (1) We can use it to build a program that computes whether one person is the grandparent of a second person. (2) We can use the definition to write a program to compute a person's grandparents. (3) We can use it to compute the grandchildren of a given person. (4) And we can use it to compute a table of grandparents and grandchildren. In traditional programming, we would write different programs for each of these tasks, and the definition of grandparent would not be *explicitly* encoded in any of these programs. In Logic Programming, the definition can be written just once, and that single definition can be used to accomplish all four tasks.

As another example of this (due to John McCarthy), consider the fact that, if two objects collide, they typically make a noise. This fact about the world can be used in designing programs for various purposes. (1) If we want to wake someone else, we can bang two objects together. (2) If we want to avoid waking someone, we would be careful *not* to let things collide. (3) If we see two cars come close in the distance and we hear a bang, we can conclude that they had collided. (4) If we see two cars come close together but we do not hear anything, we might guess that they did not collide.

1.4 APPLICATIONS OF LOGIC PROGRAMMING

Logic Programming can be used fruitfully in almost any application area. However, it has special value in application areas characterized by large numbers of definitions and constraints and rules of action, especially where those definitions and constraints and rules come from multiple sources or where they are frequently changing. The following are a few application areas where Logic Programming has proven particularly useful.

Database Systems. By conceptualizing database tables as sets of simple sentences, it is possible to use Logic in support of database systems. For example, the language of Logic can be used to define virtual views of data in terms of explicitly stored tables; it can be used to encode constraints on databases; it can be used to specify access control policies; and it can be used to write update rules.

Logical Spreadsheets/Worksheets. Logical spreadsheets (sometimes called worksheets) generalize traditional spreadsheets to include logical constraints as well as traditional arithmetic formulas. Examples of such constraints abound. For example, in scheduling applications, we might have timing constraints or restrictions on who can reserve which rooms. In the domain of travel reservations, we might have constraints on adults and infants. In academic program sheets, we might have constraints on how many courses of varying types that students must take.

Data Integration. The language of Logic can be used to relate the concepts in different vocabularies and thereby allow users to access multiple, heterogeneous data sources in an integrated fashion, giving each user the illusion of a single database encoded in his own vocabulary.

Enterprise Management. Logic Programming has special value in expressing and implementing *business rules* of various sorts. Internal business rules include enterprise policies (e.g., expense approval) and workflow (who does what and when). External business rules include the details of contracts with other enterprises, configuration and pricing rules for company products, and so forth.

Computational Law. Computational Law is the branch of Legal Informatics concerned with the representation of rule and regulations in computable form. Encoding laws in computable form enables automated legal analysis and the creation of technology to make that analysis available to citizens, and monitors and enforcers, and legal professionals.

General Game Playing. General game players are systems able to accept descriptions of arbitrary games at runtime and able to use such descriptions to play those games effectively without human intervention. In other words, they do not know the rules until the games start. Logic Programming is widely used in General Game Playing as the preferred way to formalize game descriptions.

1.5 BASIC LOGIC PROGRAMMING

Over the years, various types of Logic Programming have been explored (Basic Logic Programming, Classic Logic Programming, Transaction Logic Programming, Constraint Logic Programming, Disjunctive Logic Programming, Answer Set Programming, Inductive Logic Programming, etc.). Along with these different types of Logic Programming, a variety of logic programming languages have been developed (e.g., Datalog, Prolog, Epilog, Golog, Progol, LPS, etc.). In this volume, we concentrate on Basic Logic Programming, a variant of Transaction Logic Programming; and we use Epilog in writing our examples.

In Basic Logic Programming, we model the states of an application as sets of simple facts (called *datasets*), and we write *rules* to define abstract *views* of the facts in datasets. We model changes to state as *primitive updates* to our datasets, i.e., sets of additions and deletions of facts, and we write *rules* of a different sort to define *compound actions* in terms of primitive updates.

Epilog (the language we use in this volume) is closely related to Datalog and Prolog. Their syntaxes are almost identical. And the three languages are nicely ordered in terms of expressiveness—with Datalog being a subset of Prolog and Prolog being a subset of Epilog. For the sake of simplicity, we use the syntax of Epilog throughout this course, and we talk about the Epilog interpreter and compiler. Thus, when we mention Datalog in what follows, we are referring to the Datalog subset of Epilog; and, when we mention Prolog, we are referring to the Prolog subset of Epilog.

As we shall see, all three of these languages (Datalog and Prolog and Epilog) are less expressive than the languages associated with more complex forms of Logic Programming (such as Disjunctive Logic Programming and Answer Set Programming). While these restrictions limit what we can say in these languages, the resulting programs are computationally better behaved and, in most cases, more practical than programs written in more expressive languages. Moreover, due to these restrictions, Datalog and Prolog and Epilog are easy to understand; and, consequently, they have pedagogical value as an introduction to more complex Logic Programming languages.

In keeping with our emphasis on Basic Logic Programming, the material of the course is divided into five units. In this unit, Unit 1, we give an overview of Logic Programming and Basic Logic Programming, and we introduce *datasets*. In Unit 2, we talk about *queries* and *updates*. In Unit 3, we talk about *view definitions*. In Unit 4, we concentrate on *operation definitions*. And, in Unit 5, we talk about *variations*, i.e., other forms of Logic Programming.

HISTORICAL NOTES

In the mid-1950s, computer scientists began to concentrate on the development of high-level programming languages. As a contribution to this effort, John McCarthy suggested the language of Symbolic Logic as a candidate, and he articulated the ideal of declarative programming. He gave voice to these ideas in a seminal paper, published in 1958, which describes a type of system that he called an *advice taker*.

> "The main advantage we expect the advice taker to have is that its behavior will be improvable merely by making statements to it, telling it about its ... environment and what is wanted from it. To make these statements will require little, if any, knowledge of the program or the previous knowledge of the advice taker."

The idea of declarative programming caught the imaginations of subsequent researchers—notably Bob Kowalski, one of the fathers of Logic Programming, and Ed Feigenbaum, the inventor of Knowledge Engineering. In a paper written in 1974, Feigenbaum gave a forceful restatement of McCarthy's ideal.

> "The potential use of computers by people to accomplish tasks can be 'one-dimensionalized' into a spectrum representing the nature of the instruction that must be given the computer to do its job. Call it the what-to-how spectrum. At one extreme of the spectrum, the user supplies his intelligence to instruct the machine with precision exactly how to do his job step-by-step. ... At the other end of the spectrum is the user with his real problem. ... He aspires to communicate what he wants done ... without having to lay out in detail all necessary subgoals for adequate performance."

The development of Logic Programming in its present form can be traced to subsequent debates about declarative vs. procedural representations of knowledge in the Artificial Intelligence community.

Advocates of procedural representations were mainly centered at MIT, under the leadership of Marvin Minsky and Seymour Papert. Although it was based on the proof methods of logic, Planner, developed at MIT, was the first language to emerge within the proceduralist paradigm. Planner featured pattern-directed invocation of procedural plans from goals (i.e., goal-reduction or backward chaining) and from assertions (i.e., forward chaining). The most influential implementation of Planner was the subset of Planner, called Micro-Planner, implemented by Gerry Sussman, Eugene Charniak and Terry Winograd. It was used to implement Winograd's natural-language understanding program SHRDLU, which was a landmark at that time.

Advocates of declarative representations were centered at Stanford (associated with John McCarthy, Bertram Raphael, and Cordell Green) and in Edinburgh (associated with John Alan Robinson, Pat Hayes, and Robert Kowalski). Hayes and Kowalski tried to reconcile the logic-based declarative approach to knowledge representation with Planner's procedural approach. In 1973, Hayes developed an equational language, Golux, in which different procedures could be obtained by altering the behavior of a theorem prover. Kowalski, on the other hand, developed SLD resolution, a variant of SL-resolution, and showed how it treats implications as goal-reduction procedures. Kowalski collaborated with Colmerauer in Marseille, who developed these ideas in the design of the programming language Prolog, which was implemented in the summer and autumn of 1972. The first Prolog program, also written in 1972 and implemented in Marseille, was a French question-answering system. The use of Prolog as a practical programming language was given great momentum by the development of a compiler by David Warren in Edinburgh in 1977.

CHAPTER 2

Datasets

2.1 INTRODUCTION

Datasets are collections of facts about some aspect of the world. Datasets can be used by themselves to encode information. They can also be used in combination with logic programs to form more complex information systems, as we shall see in the coming chapters.

We begin this chapter by talking about conceptualizing the world. We then introduce a formal language for encoding information about our conceptualization in the form of datasets. We provide some examples of datasets encoded within this language. And, finally, we discuss the issues involved in reconceptualizing an application area and encoding those different conceptualizations as datasets with different vocabularies.

2.2 CONCEPTUALIZATION

When we think about the world, we usually think in terms of objects and relationships among these objects. *Objects* include things like people and offices and buildings. *Relationships* include things like parenthood, friendship, office assignments, office locations, and so forth.

One way to represent such information is in the form of graphs. As an example, consider the graph shown below. The nodes here represent objects, and the arcs represent relationships among these objects.

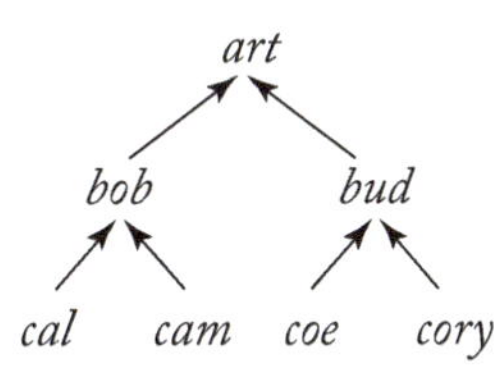

Alternatively, we can represent such information in the form of tables. For example, we can encode the information in the preceding graph as a table like the one shown below.

parent	
art	bob
art	bea
bob	cal
bob	cam
bea	coe
bea	cory

Another possibility is to encode individual relationships as sentences in a formal language. For example, we can represent our kinship information as shown below. Here, each fact takes the form of a sentence consisting of name for the relationship and the names of the entities involved.

```
parent(art,bob)
parent(art,bea)
parent(bob,cal)
parent(bob,cam)
parent(bea,coe)
parent(bea,cory)
```

While graphs and tables are intuitively appealing, a sentential representation is more useful for our purposes. So, in what follows we represent facts as sentences, and we represent different states of the world as different sets of such sentences.

A final note before we leave this discussion of conceptualization. In what follows, we use the words *relation* and *relationship* interchangeably. From a mathematical point of view, this is not exactly correct, as there is a subtle difference between the two notions. However, for our purposes, the difference is unimportant, and it is often easier to say *relation* than *relationship*.

2.3 DATASETS

A *dataset* is a collection of simple facts that characterize the state of an application area. Facts in a dataset are assumed to be true; facts that are not included in the dataset are assumed to be false. Different datasets characterize different states.

Constants are strings of lower case letters, digits, underscores, and periods *or* strings of arbitrary ASCII characters enclosed by double quotes. For reasons described in the next chapter, we prohibit strings containing uppercase letters except within double quotes. Examples of constants include `a`, `b`, `comp225`, `123`, `3.14159`, `barack_obama`, and `"Mind your p's and q's!"`. Non-examples include `Art`, `p&q`, `the-house-that-jack-built`. The first contains an upper case letter; the second contains an ampersand; and the third contains hyphens. A *vocabulary* is a collection of constants.

In what follows, we distinguish three types of constants. *Symbols* are intended to represent objects in the world. *Constructors* are used to create compound names for objects. *Predicates* represent relationships on objects.

Each constructor and predicate has an associated *arity*, i.e., the number of arguments allowed in any expression involving the constructor or predicate. *Unary* constructors and predicates are those that take one argument; *binary* constructors and predicates take two arguments; and *ternary* constructors and predicates take three arguments. Beyond that, we often say that constructors and predicates are *n-ary*. Note that it is possible to have a predicate with no arguments, representing a condition that is simply true or false.

A *ground term* is either a symbol or a compound name. A *compound name* is an expression formed from an n-ary constructor and n ground terms enclosed in parentheses and separated by commas. If `a` and `b` are symbols and `pair` is a binary constructor, then `pair(a,a)`, `pair(a,b)`, `pair(b,a)`, and `pair(b,b)` are compound names. The adjective *ground* here means that the term does not contain any *variables* (which we discuss in the next chapter).

The *Herbrand universe* for a vocabulary is the set of all ground terms that can be formed from the symbols and constructors in the vocabulary. For a finite vocabulary without constructors, the Herbrand universe is finite (i.e., just the symbols). For a finite vocabulary *with* constructors, the Herbrand universe is infinite (i.e., the symbols and all compound names that can be formed from those symbols). The Herbrand universe for the vocabulary described in the previous paragraph is shown below.

```
{pair(a,b), pair(a,pair(b,c)), pair(a,pair(b,pair(c,d))), ...}
```

A *datum/factoid/fact* is an expression formed from an n-ary predicate and n ground terms enclosed in parentheses and separated by commas. For example, if `r` is a binary predicate and `a` and `b` are symbols, then `r(a,b)` is a datum.

The *Herbrand base* for a vocabulary is the set of all factoids that can be formed from the constants in the vocabulary. For example, for a vocabulary with just two symbols `a` and `b` and the single binary predicate `r`, the Herbrand base for this language is shown below.

```
{r(a,a), r(a,b), r(b,a), r(b,b)}
```

Finally, we define a *dataset* to be any subset of the Herbrand base, i.e., an arbitrary set of facts that can be formed from the vocabulary of a database. Intuitively, we can think of the data in a dataset as the facts that we believe to be true; data that are not in the dataset are assumed to be false.

2.4 EXAMPLE – SORORITY WORLD

Consider the interpersonal relations of a small sorority. There are just four members—Abby, Bess, Cody, and Dana. Some of the girls like each other, but some do not.

Figure 2.1 shows one set of possibilities. The checkmark in the first row here means that Abby likes Cody, while the absence of a checkmark means that Abby does not like the other girls (including herself). Bess likes Cody too. Cody likes everyone but herself. And Dana also likes the popular Cody.

	Abby	Bess	Cody	Dana
Abby			✓	
Bess			✓	
Cody	✓	✓		✓
Dana			✓	

Figure 2.1: One state of Sorority World.

In order to encode this information as a dataset, we adopt a vocabulary with four symbols (`abby`, `bess`, `cody`, `dana`) and one binary predicate (`likes`). Using this vocabulary, we can encode the information in Figure 2.1 by writing the dataset shown below.

```
likes(abby,cody)
likes(bess,cody)
likes(cody,abby)
likes(cody,bess)
likes(cody,dana)
likes(dana,cody)
```

Note that the `likes` relation has no inherent restrictions. It is possible for one person to like a second without the second person liking the first. It is possible for a person to like just one other person or many people or nobody. It is possible that everyone likes everyone or no one likes anyone.

Even for a small world like this one, there are quite a few possible ways the world could be. Given four girls, there are sixteen *possible* instances of the `likes` relation—`likes(abby,abby)`, `likes(abby,bess)`, `likes(abby,cody)`, `likes(abby,dana)`, `likes(bess,abby)`, and so forth. Each of these sixteen can be either true or false. There are 2^{16} (i.e., 65,536) possible combinations of these true-false possibilities; and so there are 2^{16} possible states of this world and, therefore, 2^{16} possible datasets.

2.5 EXAMPLE - KINSHIP

As another example, consider a small dataset about kinship. The terms in this case once again represent people. The predicates name properties of these people and their relationships with each other.

In our example, we use the binary predicate `parent` to specify that one person is a parent of another. The sentences below constitute a dataset describing six instances of the `parent` relation. The person named `art` is a parent of the person named `bob` and the person named `bea`; `bob` is the parent of `cal` and `cam`; and `bea` is the parent of `coe` and `cory`.

```
parent(art,bob)
parent(art,bea)
parent(bob,cal)
parent(bob,cam)
parent(bea,coe)
parent(bea,cory)
```

The `adult` relation is a unary relation, i.e., a simple property of a person, not a relationship with other people. In the dataset below, everyone is an adult except for Art's grandchildren.

```
adult(art)
adult(bob)
adult(bea)
```

We can express gender with two unary predicates `male` and `female`. The following data expresses the genders of all of the people in our dataset. Note that, in principle, we need only one relation here, since one gender is the complement of the other. However, representing both allows us to enumerate instances of both gender equally efficiently, which can be useful in certain applications.

```
male(art)          female(bea)
male(bob)          female(coe)
male(cal)          female(cory)
male(cam)
```

As an example of a ternary relation, consider the data shown below. Here, we use `prefers` to represent the fact that the first person likes the second person more than the third person. For example, the first sentence says that Art prefers `bea` to `bob`; the second sentence says that `bob` prefers `cal` to `cam`.

```
prefers(art,bea,bob)
prefers(bob,cal,cam)
```

Note that the order of arguments in such sentences is arbitrary. Given the meaning of the `prefers` relation in our example, the first argument denotes the subject, the second argument is the person who is preferred, and the third argument denotes the person who is less preferred. We could equally well have interpreted the arguments in other orders. The important thing is consistency—once we choose to interpret the arguments in one way, we must stick to that interpretation everywhere.

One noteworthy difference difference between Sorority World and Kinship is that there is just one relation in the former (i.e., the `likes` relation), whereas there are multiple relations in the latter (three unary predicates, one binary predicate, and one ternary predicate).

A more subtle and interesting difference is that the relations in Kinship are constrained in various ways while the `likes` relation in Sorority World is not. It is possible for any person in Sorority World to like any other person; all combinations of likes and dislikes are possible. By contrast, in Kinship there are constraints that limit the number of possible states. For example, it is not possible for a person to be his own parent, and it is not possible for a person to be both male and female.

2.6 EXAMPLE – BLOCKS WORLD

The Blocks World is a popular application area for illustrating ideas in the field of Artificial Intelligence. A typical Blocks World scene is shown in Figure 2.2.

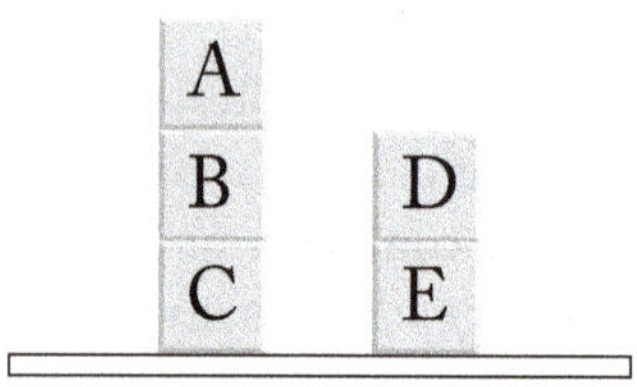

Figure 2.2: One state of Blocks World.

Most people looking at Figure 2.2 interpret it as a configuration of five toy blocks. Some people conceptualize the table on which the blocks are resting as an object as well; but, for simplicity, we ignore it here.

In order to describe this scene, we adopt a vocabulary with five symbols (`a`, `b`, `c`, `d`, `e`), with one symbol for each of the five blocks in the scene. The intent here is for each of these symbols to represent the block marked with the corresponding capital letter in the scene.

In a spatial conceptualization of the Blocks World, there are numerous meaningful relations. For example, it makes sense to talk about the relation that holds between two blocks if and only if one is resting on the other. In what follows, we use the predicate on to refer to this relation. We might also talk about the relation that holds between two blocks if and only if one is anywhere above the other, i.e., the first is resting on the second or is resting on a block that is resting on the second, and so forth. In what follows, we use the predicate `above` to talk about this relation. There is the relation that holds of three blocks that are stacked one on top of the other. We use the predicate `stack` as a name for this relation. We use the predicate `clear` to denote the relation that holds of a block if and only if there is no block on top of it. We use the predicate `table` to denote the relation that holds of a block if and only if that block is resting on the table.

The arities of these predicates are determined by their intended use. Since on is intended to denote a relation between two blocks, it has arity 2. Similarly, `above` has arity 2. The `stack` predicate has arity 3. Predicates `clear` and `table` each have arity 1.

Given this vocabulary, we can describe the scene in Figure 2.2 by writing sentences that state which relations hold of which objects or groups of objects. Let's start with on. The following sentences tell us directly for each ground relational sentence whether it is true or false.

```
on(a,b)
on(b,c)
on(d,e)
```

There are four `above` facts. The `above` relation holds of the same pairs of blocks as the on relation, but it includes one additional fact for block `a` and block `c`.

```
above(a,b)
above(b,c)
above(a,c)
above(d,e)
```

In similar fashion, we can encode the stack relation and the above relation. There is just one stack here—block `a` on block `b` and block `b` on block `c`.

```
stack(a,b,c)
```

Finally, we can write out the facts for `clear` and `table`. Blocks `a` and `d` are clear, while blocks `c` and `e` are on the table.

```
clear(a)            table(c)
clear(d)            table(e)
```

As with Kinship, the relations in Blocks World are constrained in various ways. For example, it is not possible for a block to be on itself. Moreover, some of these relations are entirely determined by others. For example, given the on relation, the facts about all of the other relations are entirely determined. In a later chapter, we see how to write out definitions for such concepts and thereby avoid having to write out individual facts for such defined concepts.

2.7 EXAMPLE – FOOD WORLD

As another example of these concepts, consider a small dataset about food and menus. The goal here is to create a dataset that lists meals that are available at a restaurant on different days of the week.

The symbols in this case come in two types - days of the week (`monday`, ... , `friday`) and different types of food (`calamari`, `vichyssoise`, `beef`, and so forth). There are three constructors—a 3-ary constructor for three course meals (`three`), a 4-ary constructor for four course meals (`four`), and a 5-ary constructor for five course meals (`five`). There is a single binary predicate `menu` that relates days of the week and available meals.

The following is an example of a dataset using this vocabulary. On Monday, the restaurant offers a three course meal with calamari and beef and shortcake, and it offers a different three course meal with puree and beef and ice cream for dessert. On Tuesday, the restaurant offers one of the same three-course meals and a four-course meal as well. On Wednesday, the restaurant offers just one meal—the four-course meal from the day before. On Thursday, the restaurant offers a five-course meal; and, on Friday, it offers a different five-course meal.

```
menu(monday,three(calamari,beef,shortcake))
menu(monday,three(puree,beef,icecream))
menu(tuesday,three(puree,beef,icecream))
menu(tuesday,four(consomme,greek,lamb,baklava))
menu(wednesday,four(consomme,greek,lamb,baklava))
menu(thursday,five(vichyssoise,caesar,trout,chicken,tiramisu))
menu(friday,five(vichyssoise,green,trout,beef,souffle))
```

Note that, although there are constructors here, the dataset is finite in size. In fact, there are strong restrictions on what sentences make sense. For example, only symbols representing days of the week appear as the first argument of the `menu` relation. Only symbols representing foods appear as arguments in compound names. And only whole meals appear as the second argument of the `menu` relation. Note also that compound names are not nested here. These kinds of restrictions are common in datasets. Later in the book, we show how we can formalize these constraints.

2.8 REFORMULATION

No matter how we choose to conceptualize the world, it is important to realize that there are other conceptualizations as well. Furthermore, there need not be any correspondence between the objects, functions, and relations in one conceptualization and the objects, functions, and relations in another.

In some cases, changing one's conceptualization of the world can make it impossible to express certain kinds of knowledge. A famous example of this is the controversy in the field of physics between the view of light as a wave phenomenon and the view of light in terms of particles. Each conceptualization allowed physicists to explain different aspects of the behavior of light, but neither alone sufficed. Not until the two views were merged in modern quantum physics were the discrepancies resolved.

In other cases, changing one's conceptualization can make it more difficult to express knowledge, without necessarily making it impossible. A good example of this, once again in the field of physics, is changing one's frame of reference. Given Aristotle's geocentric view of the universe, astronomers had great difficulty explaining the motions of the moon and other planets. The data were explained (with epicycles, etc.) in the Aristotelian conceptualization, although the explanation was extremely cumbersome. The switch to a heliocentric view quickly led to a more perspicuous theory.

This raises the question of what makes one conceptualization more appropriate than another. Currently, there is no comprehensive answer to this question. However, there are a few issues that are especially noteworthy.

One such issue is the *grain size* of the objects associated with aconceptualization. Choosing too small a grain can make knowledge formalization prohibitively tedious. Choosing too large a grain can make it impossible.

As an example of the former problem, consider a conceptualization of the scene in Blocks World in which the objects in the universe of discourse are the atoms composing the blocks in the picture. Each block is composed of enormously many atoms, so the universe of discourse is extremely large. Although it is, in principle, possible to describe the scene at this level of detail, it is senseless if we are interested in only the vertical relationship of the blocks made up of those atoms. Of course, for a chemist interested in the composition of blocks, the atomic view of the scene might be more appropriate, and our conceptualization in terms of blocks has too large a grain.

Indistinguishability abstraction is a form of object reformulation that deals with grain size. If several objects mentioned in a dataset satisfy all of the same conditions, under appropriate circumstances, it is possible to abstract the objects to a single object that does not distinguish the identities of the individuals. This can decrease the cost of processing queries by avoiding redundant computation in which the only difference is the identities of these objects.

Another way of reconceptualizing the world is the *reification* of relations as objects in the universe of discourse. The advantage of this is that it allows us to consider properties of properties.

As an example, consider a Blocks World conceptualization in which there are five blocks, no constructors, and three unary predicates, each corresponding to a different color. This conceptualization allows us to consider the colors of blocks but not the properties of those colors.

We can remedy this deficiency by *reifying* various color relations as objects in their own right and by adding a relation to associate blocks with colors. Because the colors are objects in the universe of discourse, we can then add relations that characterize them, e.g., warm, cool, and so forth.

There is also the reverse of reification, viz. *relationalization*. Combining relationalization and reification is a common way to change from one conceptualization to another.

Note that, in this discussion, no attention has been paid to the question of whether the objects in one's conceptualization of the world really exist. We have adopted neither the standpoint of *realism*, which posits that the objects in one's conceptualization really exist, nor that of *nominalism*, which holds that one's concepts have no necessary external existence. Conceptualizations are our inventions, and their justification is based solely on their utility. This lack of commitment indicates the essential ontological promiscuity of Logic Programming: any conceptualization of the world is accommodated, and we seek those that are useful for our purposes.

2.9 EXERCISES

2.1. Consider the Sorority World introduced above. Write out a dataset describing a state in which every girl likes herself and no one else.

2.2. Consider a variation of the Sorority World example in which we have a single binary relation, called `friend`. `friend` differs from `likes` in two ways. It is non-reflexive, i.e., a girl cannot be friends with herself; and it is symmetric, i.e., if one girl is a friend of a second girl, then the second girl is friends with the first. Write out a dataset describing a state that satisfies the non-reflexivity and symmetry of the `friend` relation *and* so that exactly six `friend` facts are true. Note that there are multiple ways in which this can be done.

2.3. Consider a variation of the Sorority World example in which we have a single binary relation, called `younger`. `younger` differs from `likes` in three ways. It is non-reflexive, i.e., a girl cannot be younger than herself. It is antisymmetric, i.e., if one girl is younger than a second, then the second is *not* younger than the first. It is transitive, i.e., if one girl is younger than a second and the second is younger than a third, then the first is younger than the third. Write out a dataset describing a state that satisfies the reflexivity, antisymmetry, and transitivity of the younger relation *and* so that the maximum number of `younger` facts are true. Note that there are multiple ways in which this can be done.

2.4. A person x is a *sibling* of a person y if and only if x is a brother or a sister of y. Write out the `sibling` facts corresponding to the `parent` facts shown below.

```
parent (art,bob)
parent (art,bob)
parent (art,bob)
parent (art,bob)
parent (art,bob)
parent (art,bob)
```

2.5. Consider the state of the Blocks World pictured below. Write out all of the above facts that are true in this state.

2.6. Consider a world with n symbols and a single binary predicate. How many distinct facts can be written in this language?

$$n, 2n, n^2, 2^n, n^n, 2^{n^2}, 2^{2^n}$$

2.7. Consider a world with n symbols and a single binary predicate. How many distinct datasets are possible for this language?

$$n, 2n, n^2, 2^n, n^n, 2^{n^2}, 2^{2^n}$$

2.8. Consider a world with n symbols and a single binary predicate; and suppose that the binary relation is functional, i.e., every symbol in the first position is paired with exactly one symbol in the second position. How many distinct datasets satisfy this restriction?

$$n, 2n, n^2, n^n, 2^n, 2^{n^2}, 2^{2^n}$$

PART II

Queries and Updates

CHAPTER 3

Queries

3.1 INTRODUCTION

In Chapter 2, we saw how to represent the state of an application area as a dataset. If a dataset is large, it can be difficult to answer questions based on that dataset. In this chapter, we look at various ways of *querying* a dataset to find just the information that we need.

The simplest form of query is a *true-or-false* question. Given a factoid and a dataset, we might want to know whether or not the factoid is true in that dataset. For example, we might want to know whether a person Art is the parent of Bob. Answering an atomic true-or-false question is simply a matter of checking whether the given factoid is a member of the dataset.

A more interesting form of query is a *fill-in-the-blanks* question. Given a factoid with blanks, we might want values that, when substituted for the blanks, make the query true. For example, we might want to look up the children of Art or the parents of Bill or pairs of parents and children.

An even more interesting form of query is a *compound* question. We might want values for which a Boolean combination of conditions is true. For example, we might want whether Art is the parent of Bob *or* the parent of Bud. Or we might want to find all people who have sons *and* who have *no* daughters.

We begin this chapter by looking at an extension of our dataset language that allows us to express such questions. In the next section, we define the syntax of our language; and, in the section thereafter, we define its semantics. We then look at some examples of using this language to query datasets. With that introduction behind us, we look at an important syntactic restriction, called safety. And, finally, we finish by discussing useful predefined concepts (e.g., arithmetic operators) that increase the power of our query language.

3.2 QUERY SYNTAX

The language of queries includes the language of datasets but provides some additional features that make it more expressive, viz. variables and query rules. Variables allow us to write fill-in-the-blanks queries. Query rules allow us to express compound queries, notably negations (to say that a condition is false), conjunctions (to say that several conditions are all true), and disjunctions (to say that at least one of several conditions is true).

In our query language, a *variable* is either a lone underscore or a string of letters, digits, and underscores beginning with an uppercase letter. For example, `_`, `X23`, `X_23`, and `Somebody` are all variables.

An *atomic sentence*, or *atom*, is analogous to a factoid in a dataset except that the arguments may include variables as well as symbols. For example, if `p` is a binary predicate and `a` is a symbol and `Y` is a variable, then `p(a,Y)` is an atomic sentence.

A *literal* is either an atom or a negation of an atom. A simple atom is called a *positive* literal. The negation of an atom is called a *negative* literal. In what follows, we write negative literals using the negation sign `~`. For example, if `p(a,b)` is an atom, then `~p(a,b)` denotes the negation of this atom. Both are literals.

A *query rule* is an expression consisting of a distinguished atom, called the *head* and a collection of zero or more literals, called the *body*. The literals in the body are called *subgoals*. The predicate in the head of a query rule must be a new predicate (i.e., not one in the vocabulary of our dataset), and all of the predicates in the body must be dataset predicates.

In what follows, we write rules as in the example shown below. Here, `goal(a,b)` is the head; `p(a,b) & ~q(b)` is the body; and `p(a,b)` and `~q(b)` are subgoals.

```
goal(a,b) :- p(a,b) & ~q(b)
```

As we shall see in the next section, a query rule is something like a reverse implication—it is a statement that the head of the rule (i.e., the overall goal) is true whenever the subgoals are true. For example, the rule above states that `goal(a,b)` is true *if* `p(a,b)` is true *and* `q(b)` is *not* true.

The expressive power of query rules is greatly enhanced through the use of variables. Consider, for example, the rule shown below. This is a more general version of the rule shown above. Instead of applying to just the specific objects `a` and `b` it applies to *all* objects. In this case, the rule states that `goal` is true of *any* object `X` and *any* object `Y` if `p` is true of `X` and `Y` and `q` is not true of `Y`.

```
goal(X,Y) :- p(X,Y) & ~q(Y)
```

A *query* is a non-empty, finite set of query rules. Typically, a query consists of just one rule. In fact, most Logic Programming systems do not support queries with multiple rules (at least not directly). However, queries with multiple rules are sometimes useful and do not add any major complexity, so in what follows we allow for the possibility of queries with multiple rules.

3.3 QUERY SEMANTICS

An *instance* of an expression (atom, literal, or rule) is one in which all variables have been consistently replaced by ground terms (i.e., terms without variables). For example, if we have a language with symbols a and b, then the instances of `goal(X,Y) :- p(X,Y) & ~q(Y)` are shown below.

```
goal(a,a) :- p(a,a) & ~q(a)
goal(a,b) :- p(a,b) & ~q(b)
goal(b,a) :- p(b,a) & ~q(a)
goal(b,b) :- p(b,b) & ~q(b)
```

Given this notion, we can define the result of the application of a single rule to a dataset. Given a rule r and a dataset Δ, we define $v(r,\Delta)$ to be the set of all ψ such that (1) ψ is the head of an arbitrary instance of r, (2) every positive subgoal in the instance is a member of Δ, and (3) no negative subgoal in the instance is a member of Δ.

The *extension* of a query is the set of all facts that can be "deduced" on the basis of the rules in the program, i.e., it is the union of $v(r_i, \Delta)$ for each r_i in our query.

To illustrate these definitions, consider a dataset describing a small directed graph. In the sentences below, we use symbols to designate the nodes of the graph, and we use the p relation to designate the arcs of the graph.

```
p(a,b)
p(b,c)
p(c,b)
```

Now suppose we were given the following query. Here, the predicate `goal` is defined to be true of every node that has an outgoing arc to another node and also an incoming arc from that node.

```
goal(X) :- p(X,Y) & p(Y,X)
```

Since there are two variables here and three symbols, there are nine instances of this rule, viz. the ones shown below.

```
goal(a) :- p(a,a) & p(a,a)
goal(a) :- p(a,b) & p(b,a)
goal(a) :- p(a,c) & p(c,a)
goal(b) :- p(b,a) & p(a,b)
goal(b) :- p(b,b) & p(b,b)
goal(b) :- p(b,c) & p(c,b)
```

```
goal(c) :- p(c,a) & p(a,c)
goal(c) :- p(c,b) & p(b,c)
goal(c) :- p(c,c) & p(c,c)
```

The body in the first of these instances is not satisfied. In fact, the body is true only in the sixth and eighth instances. Consequently, the extension of this query contains just the two atoms shown below.

```
goal(b)
goal(c)
```

The definition of semantics in terms of rule instances is simple and clear. However, Logic Programming systems typically do not implement query processing in this way. There are more efficient ways of computing such extensions. In subsequent chapters, we look at some algorithms of this sort.

3.4 SAFETY

A query rule is *safe* if and only if every variable that appears in the head or in any negative literal in the body also appears in at least one positive literal in the body.

The rule shown below is safe. Every variable in the head and every variable in the negative subgoal appears in a positive subgoal in the body. Note that it is okay for the body to contain variables that do not appear in the head.

```
goal(X) :- p(X,Y,Z) & ~q(X,Z)
```

By contrast, the two rules shown below are not safe. The first rule is not safe because the variable Z appears in the head but does not appear in any positive subgoal. The second rule is not safe because the variable Z appears in a negative subgoal but not in any positive subgoal.

```
goal(X,Y,Z) :- p(X,Y)
goal(X,Y,X) :- p(X,Y) & ~q(Y,Z)
```

To see why safety matters in the case of the first rule, suppose we had a database in which p(a,b) is true. Then, the body of the first rule is satisfied if we let X be a and Y be b. In this case, we can conclude that every corresponding instance of the head is true. But what should we substitute for Z? Intuitively, we could put anything there; but there could be many possibilities. While this is conceptually okay, it is practically problematic.

To see why safety matters in the second rule, suppose we had a database with just two facts, viz. p(a,b) and q(b,c). In this case, if we let X be a and Y be b and Z be anything other than c, then both subgoals are true, and we can conclude goal(a,b,a).

The main problem with this is that many people incorrectly interpret that negation as meaning there is no Z for which q(Y,Z) is true, whereas the correct reading is that q(Y,Z) needs to be false for just one value of Z. As we will see, there are various ways of expressing this second meaning without writing unsafe queries.

3.5 PREDEFINED CONCEPTS

In practical logic programming languages, it is common to predefine useful concepts. These typically include arithmetic functions (such as plus, times, max, min), string functions (such as concatenation), equality and inequality, aggregates (such as countofall), and so forth.

In Epilog, equality and inequality are expressed using the relations same and distinct. The sentence same(σ,τ) is true iff σ and τ are identical. The sentence distinct(σ,τ) is true if and only if σ and τ are different.

The evaluate relation is used to represent equations involving predefined functions. For example, we would write evaluate(plus(times(3,3),times(2,3),1),16) to represent the equation 3^2+2x3+1=16. If height is a binary predicate relating a figure and its height and if width is a binary predicate relating a figure and its width, we can define the area of the object as shown below. The area of X is A if the height of X is H and the width of X is W and A is the result of multiplying H and W.

```
goal(X,A) :- height(X,H) & width(X,W) & evaluate(times(H,W),A)
```

In logic programming languages that provide such predefined concepts, there are usually syntactic restrictions on their use. For example, if a query contains a subgoal with a comparison relation (such as same and distinct), then every variable that occurs in that subgoal must occur in at least one positive literal in the body and that occurrence must precede the subgoal with the comparison relation. If a query uses evaluate in a subgoal, then any variable that occurs in the first argument of that subgoal must occur in at least one positive literal in the body and that occurrence must precede the subgoal with the arithmetic relation. Details are typically found in the documentation of systems that supply such built-in concepts.

In practical logic programming languages, it is also common to include predefined aggregate operators, such as setofall and countofall.

Aggregate operators are typically represented as relations with special syntax. For example the following rule uses the countofall operator to request the number of a person's children. N is the number of children of X if and only if N is the count of all Y such that X is the parent of Y.

```
goal(X,N) :- person(X) & evaluate(countofall(Y,parent(X,Y)),N)
```

As with special relations, there are syntactic restrictions on their use. In particular, aggregate subgoals must be safe in that all variables in the second argument must be included in the first argument or must be used within positive subgoals of the rule containing the aggregate.

3.6 EXAMPLE – KINSHIP

Consider a variation of the Kinship application introduced in Chapter 2. In this case, our vocabulary consists of symbols (representing people) and a binary predicate `parent` (which is true of two people if and only if the person specified as the first argument is the parent of the person specified as the second argument).

Given data about parenthood expressed using this vocabulary, we can write queries to extract information about other relationships as well. For example, we can find grandparents and grandchildren by writing the query shown below. A person `X` is the grandparent of a person `Z` if `X` is the parent of a person `Y` and `Y` is the parent of `Z`. The variable `Y` here is a *thread variable* that connects the first subgoal to the second but does not itself appear in the head of the rule.

```
goal(X,Z) :- parent(X,Y) & parent(Y,Z)
```

In general, we can write queries with multiple rules. For example, we can collect all of the people mentioned in our dataset by writing the following multi-rule query. In this case the conditions are disjunctive (at least one must be true), whereas the conditions in the grandfather case are conjunctive (both must be true).

```
goal(X) :- parent(X,Y)
goal(Y) :- parent(X,Y)
```

In some cases, it is helpful to use built-in relations in our queries. For example, we can ask for all pairs of people who are siblings by writing the query rule shown below. We use the `distinct` condition here to avoid listing a person as his own sibling.

```
goal(Y,Z) :- parent(X,Y) & parent(X,Z) & distinct(Y,Z)
```

While we can express many common kinship relationships using our query language, there are some relationships that are just too difficult. For example, there is no way to ask for all ancestors of a person (parents, grandparents, great grandparents, and so forth). For this, we need the ability to write *recursive* queries. We show how to write such queries in the chapter on *view* definitions.

3.7 EXAMPLE – MAP COLORING

Consider the problem of coloring planar maps using only four colors, the idea being to assign each region a color so that no two adjacent regions are assigned the same color.

A typical map is shown below. Here we have six regions. Some are adjacent to each other, meaning that they cannot be assigned the same color. Others are not adjacent, meaning that they can be assigned the same color.

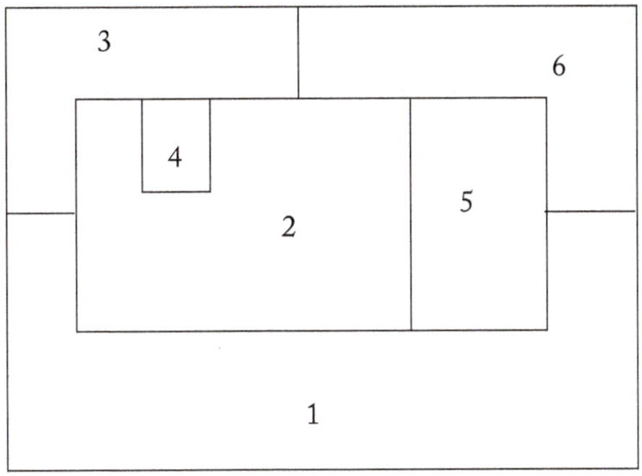

We can enumerate the hues to be used as shown below. The constants red, green, blue, and purple stand for the hues red, green, blue, and purple, respectively.

```
hue(red)
hue(green)
hue(blue)
hue(purple)
```

In the case of the map shown above, our goal is to find six hues (one for each region of the map) such that no two adjacent regions have the same hue. We can express this goal by writing the query shown below.

```
goal(C1,C2,C3,C4,C5,C6) :-
  hue(C1) & hue(C2) & hue(C3) & hue(C4) & hue(C5) & hue(C6) &
  distinct(C1,C2) & distinct(C1,C3) & distinct(C1,C5) & distinct(C1,C6) &
  distinct(C2,C3) & distinct(C2,C4) & distinct(C2,C5) & distinct(C2,C6) &
  distinct(C3,C4) & distinct(C3,C6) & distinct(C5,C6)
```

Evaluating this query will result in 6-tuples of hues that ensure that no two adjacent regions have the same color. In problems like this one, we usually want only one solution rather than all solutions. However, finding even one solution is such cases can be costly. In Chapter 4, we discuss ways of writing such queries that makes the process of finding such solutions more efficient.

3.8 EXERCISES

3.1. For each of the following strings, say whether it is a syntactically legal query.

(a) `goal(X) :- p(a,f(f(X)))`

(b) `goal(X,Y) :- p(X,Y) & ~p(Y,X)`

(c) `~goal(X,Y) :- p(X,Y) & p(Y,X)`

(d) `goal(P,Y) :- P(a,Y)`

(e) `goal(X) :- p(X,b) & p(X,p(b,c))`

3.2. Say whether each of the following queries is safe.

(a) `goal(X,Y) :- p(X,Y) & p(Y,X)`

(b) `goal(X,Y) :- p(X,Y) & p(Y,Z)`

(c) `goal(X,Y) :- p(X,X) & p(X,Z)`

(d) `goal(X,Y) :- p(X,Y) & ~p(Y,Z)`

(e) `goal(X,Y) :- p(X,Y) & ~p(Y,Y)`

3.3. What is the result of evaluating the query `goal(X,Z) :- p(X,Y) & p(Y,Z)` on the dataset shown below.

```
p(a,b)
p(a,c)
p(b,d)
p(c,d)
```

3.4. Assume we have a dataset with a binary predicate `parent` (which is true of two people if and only if the person specified as the first argument is the parent of the person specified as the second argument). Write a query that defines the property of being childless. Hint: use the aggregate operator `countofall`. And be sure your query is safe. (This exercise is not difficult, but it is slightly tricky.)

3.5. For each of the following problems, write a query to solve the problem. Values should include just the digits 8, 1, 4, 7, 3 and each digit should be used at most once in the solution of each puzzle. Your query should express the problem as stated, i.e., you should not first solve the problem yourself and then have the query simply return the answer.

(a) The product of a 1-digit number and a 2-digit number is 284.

(b) The product of two 2-digit numbers plus a 1-digit number is 3,355.

(c) The product of a 3-digit number and a 1-digit number minus a 1 digit number is 1,137.

(d) The product of a 2-digit number and a 3-digit number is between 13,000 and 14,000.

(e) When a 3-digit number is divided by a 2-digit number the result is between 4 and 6.

CHAPTER 4

Updates

4.1 INTRODUCTION

In the preceding chapter, we saw to how to write queries to extract information from a dataset. In this chapter, we look at how to update the information in a dataset, i.e., how to transform one dataset into another, ideally without rewriting all of the factoids and instead concentrating on only those factoids that have changed their truth values.

4.2 UPDATE SYNTAX

As with our query language, our update language includes the language of datasets but provides some additional features. Again, we have variables, but in this case we have update rules in place of query rules.

An *update rule* is an expression consisting of a non-empty collection of literals (called *conditions*) and a second non-empty collection of literals (called *conclusions*). The conditions and conclusions may be ground or they may contain variables. There is only one restriction: all variables in conclusions must also appear in the positive conditions.

In what follows, we write update rules as in the example shown below. Here, `p(a,b)` and `~q(b)` are conditions, and `~p(a,b)` and `p(b,a)` are conclusions.

```
p(a,b) & ~q(b) ==> ~p(a,b) & p(b,a)
```

As we shall see in the next section, an update rule is something like a condition-action rule. It is a statement that whenever the conditions are true, then the negative conclusions should be deleted from the dataset, and the positive conclusions should be added. For example, the rule above states that, *if* `p(a,b)` is true *and* `q(b)` is *not* true, then `p(a,b)` should be removed from the dataset and `p(b,a)` should be added.

As with query rules, the power of update rules is greatly enhanced through the use of variables. Consider, for example, the rule shown below. This is a more general version of the rule shown above. Instead of applying to just the specific objects `a` and `b` it applies to *all* objects.

```
p(X,Y) & ~q(Y) ==> ~p(X,Y) & p(Y,X)
```

An *update* is a finite collection of update rules. Typically, an update consists of just one rule. However, updates with multiple rules are sometimes useful and do not add any major complexity, so in what follows we allow for the possibility of updates with multiple rules.

4.3 UPDATE SEMANTICS

An *instance* of an update rule is one in which all variables have been consistently replaced by ground terms (i.e., terms without variables). For example, if we have a language with symbols a and b, then the instances of `p(X,Y) & ~q(Y) ==> ~p(X,Y) & p(Y,X)` are shown below.

```
p(a,a) & ~q(a) ==> ~p(a,a) & p(a,a)
p(a,b) & ~q(b) ==> ~p(a,b) & p(b,a)
p(b,a) & ~q(a) ==> ~p(b,a) & p(a,b)
p(b,b) & ~q(b) ==> ~p(b,b) & p(b,b)
```

Suppose we are given a dataset Δ and an update rule r. We say that an *instance* of r is *active* on Δ if and only if the conditions are all true on Δ. We define the positive update set $A(r,\Delta)$ to be the set of all positive conclusions in some active instance of r, and we define the negative update set $D(r,\Delta)$ to be the set of all negative conclusions in some active instance of r.

The positive update set $A(\Omega,\Delta)$ for a set of rules Ω on a dataset Δ is the union of the positive updates of the rules on Δ; and the negative update set $D(\Omega,\Delta)$ for Ω is the union of the negative updates of the rules on Δ.

Finally, we obtain the result of applying a set of update rules R to a dataset Δ by removing the negative updates and adding in the positive updates, i.e., the result is $\Delta - D(\Omega,\Delta) \cap A(\Omega,\Delta)$.

Let's look at some examples to illustrate this semantics. Consider the dataset shown below. In this case, there are four symbols and one binary predicate p.

```
p(a,a)
p(a,b)
p(b,c)
p(c,c)
p(c,d)
```

Now, suppose we wanted to drop all of the p factoids in our dataset in which the first and second arguments are the same. To do this, we would specify the update shown below.

```
p(X,X) ==> ~p(X,X)
```

In this case, there would be two instances in which the conditions are true. See below.

```
p(a,a) ==> ~p(a,a)
p(c,c) ==> ~p(c,c)
```

Consequently, after execution of this update, we would have the dataset shown below.

```
p(a,b)
p(b,c)
p(c,d)
```

Now suppose that we wanted to reverse the arguments of the remaining p factoids in our dataset. To do this, we would specify an update with `p(X,Y)` as a condition; we would include `p(X,Y)` as a negative conclusion; and we would specify `p(Y,X)` as a positive conclusion. In this case, we would have one variable assignment for every factoid in our dataset; the negative conclusions would be {`p(a,b)`, `p(b,c)`, `p(c,d)`}, i.e., every factoid in our dataset; and the positive conclusions would be {`p(b,a)`, `p(c,b)`, `p(d,c)`}.

```
p(X,Y) ==> ~p(X,Y) & p(Y,X)
```

After executing this update on the preceding dataset, we would have the dataset shown below.

```
p(b,a)
p(c,d)
p(d,c)
```

4.4 SIMULTANEOUS UPDATES

Note that it sometimes happens that a factoid appears as both a positive and a negative update. As an example of this, consider an update with `p(X,a)` as condition, with `p(X,a)` as a negative conclusion and with `p(a,X)` as a positive conclusion.

```
p(X,a) ==> ~p(X,a) & p(a,X)
```

In the case of the first dataset shown in the preceding section, `p(a,a)` would appear as both a positive and a negative update.

In such cases, our semantics dictates that the factoid be removed and then added right back in again, with the result that there is no change. This is a relatively arbitrary resolution to the conflict in such cases, but it appears to be the one favored most often by programmers.

4.5 EXAMPLE – KINSHIP

Once again consider the Kinship application; and assume, as before, that we start with a single binary predicate parent (which is true of two people if and only if the person specified as the first argument is the parent of the person specified as the second argument).

The factoids shown below constitute a dataset using this vocabulary. The person named art is a parent of the person named bob and the person named bea; bob is the parent of cal and cam; and bea is the parent of coe and cory.

```
parent(art,bob)
parent(art,bea)
parent(bob,cal)
parent(bob,cam)
parent(bea,cat)
parent(bea,coe)
```

In Chapter 3, we saw how to write queries to characterize other kinship relations in terms of parent. In some cases, we might want to store the resulting factoids so that they can be accessed without recomputing.

Suppose, for example, we wanted to store information about grandparents and their grandchildren. We could do this by writing an update like the one shown below.

```
parent(X,Y) & parent(Y,Z) ==> grandparent(X,Z)
```

Starting with the dataset shown above, applying this update would result in the addition of the following factoids to our dataset.

```
grandparent(art,cal)
grandparent(art,cam)
grandparent(art,cat)
grandparent(art,coe)
```

If we subsequently wanted to remove these factoids, we could execute the update shown below, and we would end up back where we started.

```
grandparent(X,Y) ==> ~grandparent(X,Z)
```

Now, suppose we wanted to reverse the arguments to the parent predicate, relating children and parents rather than relating parents and children. To do this, we could write the following update.

```
parent(X,Y) ==> ~parent(X,Y) & parent(Y,X)
```

Executing this update would result in the following dataset.

```
parent(bob,art)
parent(bea,art)
parent(cal,bob)
parent(cam,bob)
parent(cat,bea)
parent(coe,bea)
```

In understanding updates like this one, it is important to keep in mind that updates happen *atomically*—we first compute all factoids to be changed and we then make those changes all at once—before considering any other updates.

4.6 EXAMPLE - COLORS

Ruby Red, Willa White, and Betty Blue meet for lunch. One is wearing a red skirt; one is wearing a white skirt; and one is wearing a blue skirt. No one is wearing more than one color, and no two are wearing the same color. Betty Blue tells one of her companions, "Did you notice we are all wearing skirts with different colors from our names?"; and the other woman, who is wearing a white skirt, says,"Wow, that's right!" Our job is to figure out which woman is wearing which skirt.

One way to solve problems like this is to enumerate possibilities and check, for each, whether it satisfies the constraints in the statement of the problem. This approach works, but it often requires a good deal of search. To make the process of finding solutions more efficient, we can sometimes use values we already know to infer additional values and thereby cut down on the number of possibilities we need to consider. In this section, we see how we can use updates to implement this technique. In this very special case, as we shall see, this technique eliminates search altogether.

To solve the problem, we adopt a vocabulary with six symbols `r`, `w`, `b`, `v`, `x`, and `e`. The first three denote people/colors and the latter three denote "truth values"—true, false, and unknown. To express the state of our problem, we use a ternary relation constant `c`. For example, we would write `c(r,b,v)` to mean that Ruby Red is wearing a white skirt; we would write `c(r,b,x)` to mean that Ruby Red is not wearing a white skirt; and we would write `c(r,b,e)` to mean that we do not know whether or not Ruby Red wearing a white skirt.

In solving this problem we start with the dataset shown below. Initially, we know nothing about who is wearing what.

```
c(r,r,e)
c(r,w,e)
c(r,b,e)
c(w,r,e)
c(w,w,e)
c(w,b,e)
c(b,r,e)
c(b,w,e)
c(b,b,e)
```

We can picture this situation as shown below, with the idea that the value in each cell is an indication of our belief about whether the person listed as the first argument in one of our c factoids is wearing a skirt with the color specified as the second argument. For the sake of clarity, we leave cells empty when they have value e.

	r	w	b
r			
w			
b			

First we apply the constraint that none of the women is wearing a skirt with the same color as her name.

```
c(C,C,e) ==> ~c(C,C,e) & c(C,C,x)
```

After this update, we are left with the state of affairs shown below. We now have x values along the diagonal, but we still have empty cells everywhere else.

	r	w	b
r	×		
w		×	
b			×

Next we take into account Betty Blue's comment to someone who is wearing a white skirt, which means that Betty Blue is not wearing a white skirt.

```
color(b,w,e) ==> ~color(b,w,e) & color(b,w,x)
```

This leaves us with the situation shown below.

	r	w	b
r	×		
w		×	
b		×	×

Now we get to the interesting part. First, we have updates that tell us that, if there are two occurrences of x in a row or a column and the remaining cell is an e, then the final possibility in that row or column must be a v.

```
c(P,C1,x) & c(P,C2,x) & c(P,C3,b) ==> ~c(P,C3,b) & c(P,C3,v)
c(P1,C,x) & c(P2,C,x) & c(P3,C,b) ==> ~c(P3,C,b) & c(P3,C,v)
```

Applying these updates once to the situation above leads to the situation depicted below. Here we use a green check to represent the value v. Since neither Willa White nor Betty Blue is wearing a white skirt, Ruby Red must be wearing white.

	r	w	b
r	×	✓	
w		×	
b		×	×

Similarly, we have updates that tell us that, if there is an occurrence of an v in a row or a column and there is a cell containing an e, then that e should be changed to an x.

```
c(P,C1,v) & c(P,C2,e) ==> ~c(P,C2,e) & c(P,C2,x)
c(P1,C,v) & c(P2,C,e) ==> ~c(P2,C,e) & c(P2,C,x)
```

Applying these updates gives us more information. Since Ruby Red is wearing a red skirt, she must not be wearing a blue skirt.

	r	w	b
r	×	✓	×
w		×	
b		×	×

Applying these updates three more times leads to an overall solution to the problem. Since neither Ruby Red nor Betty Blue is wearing blue, Willa White must be wearing blue. Therefore, Willa White cannot be wearing red. And, therefore, Betty Blue must be wearing red.

	r	w	b
r	×	✓	×
w	×	×	✓
b	✓	×	×

This problem is special in that we can solve it solely by inferring values from other values. In *constraint satisfaction problems* like this one, some search is often necessary. That said, *constraint propagation* techniques, like the one used here, can often cut down on this search even when they cannot be used to solve the problem altogether.

This case is also special in that it is easy to express all of the update rules necessary to solve the problem. For some problems, such as solving Sudoku puzzles, it is impractical to write update rules using our limited update language. Luckily, as we shall see in future chapters, we *can* easily express more complicated rules once we have the ability to write view definitions and action definitions.

4.7 EXERCISES

4.1. For each of the following strings, say whether it is a syntactically legal update.

(a) `p(a,f(f(X))) ==> p(X,Y)`

(b) `P(a,Y) ==> P(Y,a)`

(c) `p(X,Y) & p(Y,Z) ==> ~(X,Y) & ~p(Y,Z) & p(X,Z)`

(d) `p(X,b) ==> f(X,f(b,c))`

4.2. What is the result of applying the update rule `p(X,Y) ==> ~p(X,Y) & p(Y,X)` to the dataset shown below?

```
p(a,a)
p(a,b)
p(b,a)
```

4.3. Suppose we have a kinship dataset with a binary predicate `parent` and a unary predicate `male`. Write update rules to *replace* all factoids using the `parent` predicate with equivalent factoids using the binary predicates `father` and `mother`.

4.4. Amy, Bob, Coe, and Dan are traveling to different places. One goes by train, one by car, one by plane, and one by ship. Amy hates flying. Bob rented his vehicle. Coe tends to get seasick. And Dan loves trains. Write update rules to solve this problem by constraint propagation.

CHAPTER 5

Query Evaluation

5.1 INTRODUCTION

In Chapter 3, we described the semantics of queries in terms of instances of query rules. While the definition is easy to understand and mathematically precise, enumerating instances is not a practical method for computing answers to queries. In this chapter, we present an algorithm that produces the same results but in a more efficient manner.

We begin this chapter with a discussion of evaluation of queries without variables. In Section 5.3, we look at a way of comparing expressions containing variables. In the section after that, we show how to combine that technique with the procedure described here to produce an evaluation procedure for queries with variables. We close with an analysis of the computational complexity of our evaluation algorithm.

5.2 EVALUATING GROUND QUERIES

If a query contains multiple query rules, we check whether the body of each rule is true. If so, we add the head of the rule to the extension of our query. The procedure for determining whether the body is true depends on the type of the body.

1. If the body of a query rule is a single atom, we check whether that atom is contained in our dataset. If so, the body is true.

2. If the body is a negated atom, we check whether the atom is contained in our dataset. If so, the body is false. If the atom is *not* contained in our dataset, then the body is true.

3. If the body is a conjunction of literals, we first execute this procedure on the first conjunct. If the answer is true, we move on to the next conjunct and so forth until we are done. If the answer to any one of the conjuncts is false, then the value of the body as a whole is false.

Consider the dataset shown below. There are four symbols `a`, `b`, `c`, and `d`; and there is a single binary predicate `p`.

```
p(a,b)
p(b,c)
p(c,d)
```

Now, imagine that we are asked to evaluate the query shown below. In this case there are three rules. To compute all answers, we execute our procedure on each of these rules.

```
goal(a) :- p(a,c)
goal(b) :- p(a,b) & p(b,a)
goal(c) :- p(c,d) & ~p(d,c)
```

In the first rule, the body `p(a,c)` is an atom, so we just check whether or not it is in the dataset. Since it is not there, nothing is contributed to our result.

The body of the second rules is a conjunction `p(a,b) & p(b,a)`, and so we evaluate the conjuncts in order to see whether they are all true. In this case, the first conjunct is true but the second is false, so the conjunction as a whole is false and again nothing is contributed to our result.

The body of the third rule is also a conjunction `p(c,d) & ~p(d,c)`. Again, we check the conjuncts in turn. `p(c,d)` is true, so we move on to `~p(d,c)`. `p(d,c)` is false so the negation is true. Since both conjuncts of the conjunction are true, the conjunction as a whole is true. Consequently, we add the head of our rule `goal(c)` to our result.

5.3 MATCHING

Matching is the process of determining whether a *pattern* (an expression with or without variables) matches an instance (an expression without variables), i.e., whether the two expressions can be made identical by appropriate substitutions for the variables in the pattern.

A *substitution* is a finite set of *bindings* of variables to terms. In what follows, we write substitutions as sets of replacement rules, like the one shown below. In each rule, the variable to which the arrow is pointing is to be replaced by the term from which the arrow is pointing. In this case, `X` is associated with `a` and `Y` is associated with `b`.

$$\{X \leftarrow a,\ Y \leftarrow b\}$$

The result of *applying* a substitution σ to an expression ϕ is the expression $\phi\sigma$ obtained from ϕ by replacing every occurrence of every variable with a binding in the substitution by the term to which it is bound.

$$p(X,b)\{X \leftarrow a,\ Y \leftarrow b\} = p(a,b)$$
$$q(X,Y,X)\{X \leftarrow a,\ Y \leftarrow b\} = q(a,b,a)$$

A substitution is a *matcher* for a pattern and an instance if and only if applying the substitution to the pattern results in the given instance. One good thing about our language is that there is a simple and inexpensive procedure for computing a matcher of a pattern and an expression if it exists.

The procedure assumes a representation of expressions as sequences of subexpressions. For example, the expression `p(X,b)` can be thought of as a sequence with three elements, viz. the predicate `p`, the variable `X`, and the symbol `b`.

We start the procedure with two expressions and a substitution (which is initially empty). We then recursively process the two expressions, comparing the subexpressions at each point. Along the way, we expand the substitution with variable assignments as described below.

1. If the pattern is a symbol and the instance is the same symbol, then the procedure succeeds, returning the unmodified substitution as result.

2. If the pattern is a symbol and the instance is a different symbol or a compound expression, then the procedure fails.

3. If the pattern is a variable with a binding, we compare the binding for the variable with the given instance. If they are identical, the procedure succeeds, returning the unmodified substitution as result; otherwise it fails.

4. If the pattern is a variable without a binding, we include a binding for the variable in the given instance and we return that substitution as a result.

5. If the pattern is a compound expression and the instance is a compound expression of the same length, we iterate across the pattern and the instance.

6. If the pattern is a compound expression and the instance is a symbol or a compound expression of a different length, the procedure fails.

If we fail to match a sub-pattern and a sub-instance at any point in this process, the procedure as a whole fails. If we finish this recursive comparison of the pattern and the instance, the procedure as a whole succeeds and the accumulated substitution at that point is the resulting matcher.

As an example of this procedure in operation, consider the process of matching the pattern `p(X,Y)` and the instance `p(a,b)` with the initial substitution {}. A trace of the execution of the procedure for this case is shown below. We show the beginning of a comparison with a line labeled Compare together with the expressions being compared and the input substitution. We show the result of each comparison with a line labeled `Result`. The indentation shows the depth of recursion of the procedure.

Compare: p(X,Y), p(a,b), {}

Compare: p, p, {}

Result: {}

Compare: X, a, {}

Result: {X←a}

Compare: Y, b, {X←a}

Result: {X←a, Y←b}

Result: {x←a, y←b}

As another example, consider the process of matching the pattern p(X,X) and the instance p(a,a). A trace is shown below. By the time we compare the last arguments in the two expressions, X is bound to a, so the match succeeds.

Compare: p(X,X), p(a,a), {}

Compare: p, p, {}

Result: {}

Compare: X, a, {}

Result: {X←a}

Compare: X, a, {X←a}

Result: {X←a}

Result: {X←a}

As a final example, consider the process of trying to match the pattern p(X,X) and the expression p(a,b). The main interest in this example comes in comparing the last argument in the two expressions, viz. X and b. By the time we reach this point, X is bound to a and the corresponding instance is b. Since the pattern is a symbol and the instance is a different symbol, the match attempt fails.

Compare: p(X,X), p(a,b), {}

Compare: p, p, {}

Result: {}

Compare: X, a, {}

Result: {X←a}

Compare: X, b, {X←a}

Result: false

Result: false

This matching procedure is quite simple. However, it is worth understanding thoroughly, as it is the basis for more complicated matching procedures defined and used in later chapters.

5.4 EVALUATING QUERIES WITH VARIABLES

Evaluating queries with variables is complicated by the fact that there can be *multiple* variable bindings that make the body of a rule true; and, consequently, there can be multiple possible answers. In some cases, we want just a single answer; in some cases, we want several answers; and, in other cases, we want all answers. In what follows, we talk about a procedure for generating all answers. The procedures for the other cases are analogous.

In finding the extension for an arbitrary query rule (i.e., one with or without variables), we start with the query rule and an empty substitution. Rather than simply checking whether the body is true or false, as in the ground case, we compute the set of all variable bindings for which the body is true and, for each of these, we include in our extension the result of applying that variable binding to the head of the rule. The procedure for computing these variable bindings depends on the type of the body of the rule.

1. If the body of the rule is an atom, we try matching the atom to the factoids in our dataset. For each factoid that matches the atom, we add the corresponding substitution to our answer set; and we return the set of all substitutions obtained in this way.

2. If the query is a negation, we execute our procedure on the argument of the negation and the given substitution. If the result is a non-empty set (i.e., there are substitutions that work), then the negation is false and we return false as answer. If the result of the recursive execution is the empty set (i.e., there are no substitutions that work), then the negation as a whole is true and we return the singleton set containing the given substitution as a result.

3. If our query is a conjunction, we execute our procedure on the first conjunct and the given substitution. We then iterate over the list of answers, for each substitution executing the procedure on the remaining conjuncts and that substitution and return the resulting substitutions.

To illustrate this procedure, consider the dataset shown below.

```
p(a,b)
p(a,c)
p(b,c)
p(c,d)
```

Now, consider the query `goal(Y) :- p(a,Y)`. The pattern `p(a,Y)` matches two factoids in our dataset, and so there are two results.

```
goal(b)
goal(c)
```

Suppose instead we had the query rule `goal(Y) :- p(a,Y) & p(Y,d)`. Once again, the pattern `p(a,Y)` matches just two factoids in our dataset. Given {Y←b}, the pattern `p(Y,d)` does not match any factoids; given {Y←c}, the pattern `p(Y,d)` matches just `p(c,d)`. Thus, there is just one answer in this case.

```
goal(c)
```

Given the conjunctive query `goal(Y) :- p(a,Y) & ~p(Y,d)`, we would again find two answers to the first conjunct, viz. {Y←b} and {Y←c}. Given the first of these, the negation `~p(Y,d)` is satisfied, and so the conjunction is true. Given the second answer to the first conjunct, the negation fails and so there is no answer in this case. As with the last query, there is just one answer.

```
goal(b)
```

Finally, for a query with more than one rule, we would get the union of the answers to the individual rules.

5.5 COMPUTATIONAL ANALYSIS

One nice feature of our query evaluation algorithm is that computational analysis is straightforward. In this section, we assume a standard left-to-right implementation of evaluation with no *indexing* of datasets and no *caching* of results once they are computed.

Consider the query shown below.

```
goal(a,c) :- p(a,Y) & p(Y,c)
```

What is the cost of evaluating this query? In the worst case, there are *n*^2 facts in the database, where *n* is the number of ground terms in our language. So, we need *n*^2 steps to evaluate the first conjunct. There are at most *n* facts that have a as first argument. For each of these, we look at *n*^2 possibilities for the second conjunct. Hence, the cost of computing the instance can be expressed as shown below.

$$n^2 + n^*n^2 = n^2 + n^3$$

Now consider the general version of this query shown below.

```
goal(X,Z) :- p(X,Y) & p(Y,Z)
```

What is the cost of computing *all* answers to this query? In the worst case, there are n^2 facts in the database, where n is the number of objects in the domain. So, we need n^2 steps to evaluate the first subgoal. There are at most n^2 possible values for `Y`. For each of these, we look at n^2 possibilities for the second subgoal. The resulting cost is shown below.

$$n^2 + n^2 * n^2 = n^2 + n^4$$

Before leaving our analysis of complexity, it is instructive to compare the cost of computing answers using this algorithm with the cost of computing answers in accordance with the semantics described in the preceding chapter, i.e., by enumerating all instances of rules and, for each such instance, checking whether the body of each such instance is true or false.

In the preceding example, the query has just three variables. Consequently, for a domain with n objects, there are n^3 instances. To evaluate each of these instances, we must compare each of our two subgoals to every factoid in our dataset, and in the worst case there are n^2 of these. The overall cost is shown below.

$$n^3(n^2 + n^2) = n^5 + n^5 = 2n^5$$

Our algorithm is clearly better in this case, and the relative benefits are greater when we consider sparse datasets, i.e., datasets that do not include all possible factoids. In such cases, the "semantics-based" algorithm must still look at all instances, but our algorithm needs to look at only those instances that are derived form factoids in the dataset.

Note that, in the presence of dataset indexing or caching of results, the details of these analyses are likely to be different, but the style of analysis is the same and the relative merits of the two algorithms are more or less the same.

5.6 EXERCISES

5.1. For each of the following patterns and instances, say whether the instance matches the pattern and, if so, give the corresponding matcher.

(a) `p(X,Y)` and `p(a,a)`

(b) `p(X,Y)` and `p(a,f(a))`

(c) `p(X,f(Y))` and `p(a,f(a))`

(d) `p(X,X)` and `p(2,min(2,4))`

(e) `p(X,min(2,4))` and `p(2,2)`

5.2. Suppose that we want to find all `goal(X,Y,Z)` such that `p(X,Y) & q(Y,Z)`. Select the formula that captures the worst case complexity of our standard evaluation algorithm for this query (assuming no indexing of the dataset). The symbol n here represents the total number of objects in the domain.

(a) $2n^2 + 2n^3$

(b) $2n^2 + 2n^4$

(c) $2n^2 + n^3 + n^4$

5.3. For each of the queries shown below, select the expression that captures the worst case complexity of our standard evaluation algorithm without indexing. The symbol n represents the total number of objects in the domain.

```
goal(X,Y) :- p(X,Y) & q(Y) & q(Z)
```

(a) $n^4 + n^3 + n^2 + n$

(b) $2n^4 + 2n^3 + n^2 + n$

(c) $2n^4 + 2n^3$

```
goal(X,Y) :- p(X,Y) & q(Y)
```

(a) $n^4 + n^3 + n^2 + n$

(b) $2n^4 + 2n^3 + n^2 + n$

(c) $2n^4 + 2n^3$

CHAPTER 6

View Optimization

6.1 INTRODUCTION

Two queries are *semantically equivalent* if and only if they produce identical results for every dataset. In such cases, it does not matter which query we write if all we care about is getting the right answers. On the other hand, it is possible that one query is *computationally better* than another in that our evaluation algorithm gets those answers more quickly.

In this chapter, we look at a variety of techniques for optimizing queries, i.e., converting expensive queries into semantically equivalent queries that are computationally less complex. We begin with a discussion of subgoal ordering within query rules. We then look at eliminating useless subgoals. And we finish with a discussion of eliminating rules from queries with multiple rules.

6.2 SUBGOAL ORDERING

One very common source of inefficiency in evaluation stems from non-optimal ordering of subgoals within queries. The good news is that it is often possible to find better orderings just by looking at the form of the queries involved even without looking at the data to which the queries are applied.

As an example of inefficiency due to poor subgoal ordering, consider the query shown below. Our `goal` is true of `X` and `Y` if `p` is true of `X` and `r` is true of `X` and `Y` and `q` is true of `X`.

```
goal(X,Y) :- p(X) & r(X,Y) & q(X)
```

Intuitively, this seems like a bad way to write this query for our usual evaluation procedure. It seems as though the `q` condition should come before the `r` condition, as in the following query.

```
goal(X,Y) :- p(X) & q(X) & r(X,Y)
```

In fact, there is good reason for this intuition. For our standard evaluation procedure, the worst-case cost of evaluating the first query is n^4, where n is the size of the domain of objects. By contrast, the worst-case cost of evaluating the second query is just n^3.

Let's look at these two cases in more detail. In the worst case, there are $n^2 + 2n$ facts in the database, where n is the number of objects in the domain.

In evaluating the first query, our algorithm would first examine all $n^2 + 2n$ facts to find those that match `p(X)`. There would be at most n answers. For each of these, the algorithm would again look at $n^2 + 2n$ facts to find those that match `r(X,Y)`. There would be n for each value of `X`. Finally, for each of these pairs, the algorithm would again examine at $n^2 + 2n$ facts to find those that match `q(X)`. The grand total is shown below.

$$(n^2 + 2n) + n*((n^2 + 2n) + n*(n^2 + 2n)) = n^4 + 3n^3 + 3n^2 + 2n$$

In evaluating the second query, the algorithm would again examine all $n^2 + 2n$ facts to find those that match `p(X)`. There would be at most n answers. For each of these, the algorithm would again look at $n^2 + 2n$ facts to find those that match `q(X)`. There would be at least one for each value of `X`. Finally, for each such `X`, the algorithm would examine $n^2 + 2n$ facts to find those that match `r(X,Y)`. The grand total is shown below.

$$(n^2 + 2n) + n*((n^2 + 2n) + 1*(n^2 + 2n)) = 2n^3 + 5n^2 + 2n$$

Suppose, for example, there were 4 objects in the domain. In this case, there would be at most 4 `p` facts and 4 `q` facts and 16 `r` facts. Evaluating the first query would require 504 matches, while evaluating the second query would require only 208.

In the presence of indexing, the asymptotic complexity is the same for both orderings. However, the lower degree terms for the second ordering suggest that it is still the better ordering. Moreover, it is possible to show that, averaging over all possible databases, the second query is better than the first.

Fortunately, there is a simple method for reordering subgoals in situations like this. The basic idea is to assemble a new body for the query incrementally, picking a subgoal on each step and removing it from the list of remaining subgoals to be considered. In making its choice, the method examines the remaining subgoals in left-to-right order. If it encounters a subgoal all of whose variables are bound by subgoals already chosen, then that subgoal is added to the new query and removed from the list of remaining subgoals. If not, the method removes the first remaining subgoal from the list, adds it to the new query, updates its list of bound variables, and moves on to the next step.

As an example of this method in action, consider the first query shown above. At the start, the list of remaining subgoals consists of all three subgoals in the query. At this point, none of the three subgoals is ground, so the method chooses the first subgoal `p(X)`, adds it to its new query, and puts `X` on the list of bound variables. On the second step, the method looks at the remaining two subgoals. The subgoal `r(X,Y)` contains the unbound variable `Y` and so it is not chosen. By contrast, all of the variables in the subgoal `q(X)` are bound, so the method outputs this subgoal next. On the third step, the final subgoal is added forming the second query shown above.

6.3 SUBGOAL REMOVAL

Another common source of inefficiency in evaluation stems from the presence of redundant subgoals within queries. In many cases, it is possible to detect and eliminate such redundancies.

As a simple example of the problem, consider the query shown below. Relation `goal` is true of `X` and `Y` if `p` is true of `X` and `Y` and `q` is true of `Y` and `q` is also true of some `Z`.

```
goal(X,Y) :- p(X,Y) & q(Y) & q(Z)
```

It should be clear that the subgoal `q(Z)` is redundant here. If there is a value for `Y` such that `q(Y)` is true, then that value for `Y` also works as a value for `Z`. Consequently, we can drop the `q(Z)` subgoal (while retaining `q(Y)`), resulting in the query shown below.

```
goal(X,Y) :- p(X,Y) & q(Y)
```

Note that the opposite is not true. If we were to drop `q(Y)` and retain `q(Z)`, we would lose the constraint on the second argument of `p`, which is also an argument to `r`.

Fortunately, it is easy to determine which subgoals can be removed and which need to be retained. The basic idea is to assemble a new body for the query incrementally, picking a subgoal on each step, checking for redundancy, and adding the subgoal once if it is not redundant.

As an illustration of this method in action, consider the example shown above. The method first computes the variables in the head of the query, viz. `[X,Y]` and initializes the variable `newquery` to a new query with the same head as the original query. It then iterates over the body of the query, adding subgoals to the new query once they are checked for redundancy.

On the first step of the iteration, the method focusses on `p(X,Y)`. It creates a dataset consisting of instances of the remaining subgoals, viz. `q(x1)` and `q(x2)`; it then tries to derive `p(x0,x1)`; and, in this case, it fails. So `p(X,Y)` is added to the new query.

On the second step, the method focusses on `q(Y)`. It creates a dataset consisting of instances of the remaining subgoals, viz. `p(x0,x1)` and `q(x2)`; it then tries to derive `q(x1)`; and, once again, it fails. So `q(Y)` is added to the new query.

Finally, the method focusses on `q(Z)`. It creates a dataset consisting of instances of the other subgoals, viz. `p(x0,x1)` and `q(x1)`; it then tries to derive an instance of `q(Z)`. Note that `Z` is not bound here since it does not occur as a head variable or a variable in any of the other subgoals. In this case, the test succeeds; and so `q(Z)` is *not* added to the new query.

This method is sound in that it removes only redundant subgoals. As a result, any query produced by this method is equivalent to the query it is given as input.

Unfortunately, the method is not complete. There are redundant subgoals that it is does not detect. The problem arises when multiple redundant subgoals share variables that prevent the method from detecting the redundancy.

As an example, consider the query shown below. The relation `goal` is true of `X` if `p` is true of `X` and `Y` and `q` is true of `X` and `Y` and `p` is true of `X` and `Z` and `q` is true of `X` and `Z`.

```
goal(X) :- p(X,Y) & q(X,Y) & p(X,Z) & q(X,Z)
```

Clearly, the last two subgoals are redundant with the first two subgoals. Unfortunately, our method does not detect that either of the subgoals in either pair is redundant because of the variables shared with the other subgoal of the pair. Try it.

Detecting this sort of redundancy can be done mechanically by considering subsets of subgoals and not just individual subgoals. However, this is more expensive than the simple method outlined above.

6.4 RULE REMOVAL

An analogous form of inefficiency in evaluation stems from the presence of redundant rules. As with redundant subgoals within rules, it is often easy to detect and eliminate such redundancies.

As an example of the problem, consider the rules shown below. Relation `goal` is true of `X` if `p` is true of `X` and `Y` and `q` is true of `b` and `r` is true of `Z`. Relation `goal` is true of `X` if `p` is true of `X` and `Y` and `q` is true of `Y`.

```
goal(X) :- p(X,b) & q(b) & r(Z)
goal(X) :- p(X,Y) & q(Y)
```

Any answer produced by the first rule here is also produced by the second rule, so the first rule is redundant and can be eliminated.

The trick to detecting such redundancies is to recognize that the second rule *subsumes* the first, i.e., all of the answers produced by the second rule are produced by the first rule. If we replace some or all of the variables in the body the second rule that do not occur in the head, then the heads remain the same and all of its subgoals are members of the body of the first rule. In this case, all we need to do is to replace `Y` by `b`, and we get the rule `goal(X) :- p(X,b) & q(b)`, which is the same as the first rule except with fewer subgoals. Every output of the first rule is, therefore, an output of the second; and, consequently, the first rule can be dropped.

6.5 EXAMPLE – CRYPTARITHMETIC

A *cryptarithmetic problem* is a constraint satisfaction problem characterized by a finite set of letters and a finite set of numbers and an arithmetic constraint written in terms of the letters. A solution to the problem is a 1–1 mapping of letters to numbers such that, when the letters are replaced by their corresponding numbers, the arithmetic constraint is satisfied.

A classic cryptarithmetic is shown below. Here, the letters are {S, E, N, D, M, O, R, Y} and the numbers are the digits from 0–9 and we are looking for an assignment of the letters to digits such that the equation holds.

```
 SEND

+MORE

MONEY
```

We can formulate this problem up as a query in much the same way that we formalized the map coloring problem presented in Chapter 3. First, we have a dataset listing the allowable digits.

```
digit(0)
digit(1)
digit(2)
digit(3)
digit(4)
digit(5)
digit(6)
digit(7)
digit(8)
digit(9)
```

Next, we write a query listing the eight letters as goal values, with subgoals to fix the ranges of these variables, disjointness constraints, and additional constraints to capture the arithmetic conditions. See below. In the interest of conciseness here, we have used ordinary arithmetic operators in place of the corresponding builtins, e.g., we have used `E!=S` for used `distinct(E,S)`, and we have used used `1000*S` for `times(1000,S)`.

```
goal(S,E,N,D,M,O,R,Y) :-
  digit(S) & digit(E) & digit(N) & digit(D) &
  digit(M) & digit(O) & digit(R) & digit(Y) &
  S!=0 & E!=S & N!=S & N!=E & D!=S & D!=E & D!=N &
  M!=0 & M!=S & M!=E & M!=N & M!=D &
  O!=S & O!=E & O!=N & O!=D & O!=M &
  R!=S & R!=E & R!=N & R!=D & R!=M & R!=O &
  Y!=S & Y!=E & Y!=N & Y!=D & Y!=M & Y!=O & Y!=R &
  evaluate(1000*S+100*E+10*N+D),Send) &
  evaluate(1000*M+100*O+10*R+E),More) &
  evaluate(10000*M+1000*O+100*N+10*E+Y),Money) &
  evaluate(plus(Send,More,Money)/td>
```

Having expressed our goal in this way, we can use our evaluation procedure to generate the answer to this problem. However, this is not without difficulty. Given the way this query is written, the evaluation process will take a long time. There are 10^8 = 100,000,000 possible variable bindings. In the worst case (where there is no solution), it would check all of these. On average, it would have to look at a substantial fraction.

The good news is that we can use subgoal ordering to transform this query into one that is easier to evaluate. We simply move the inequalities up to the point where the variables are bound. See below.

```
goal(S,E,N,D,M,O,R,Y) :-
  digit(S) & S!=0 &
  digit(E) & E!=S &
  digit(N) & N!=S & N!=E &
  digit(D) & D!=S & D!=E & D!=N &
  digit(M) & M!=0 & M!=S & M!=E & M!=N & M!=D &
  digit(O) & O!=S & O!=E & O!=N & O!=D & O!=M &
  digit(R) & R!=S & R!=E & R!=N & R!=D & R!=M & R!=O &
  digit(Y) & Y!=S & Y!=E & Y!=N & Y!=D & Y!=M & Y!=O & Y!=R &
  evaluate(1000*S+100*E+10*N+D),Send) &
  evaluate(1000*M+100*O+10*R+E),More) &
  evaluate(10000*M+1000*O+100*N+10*E+Y),Money) &
  evaluate(plus(Send,More,Money)/td>
```

Having done this, we eliminate many of the possibilities before they are even generated. The upshot is that this query takes orders of magnitude less time to evaluate, on most computers taking no more than a fraction of a second.

6.6 EXERCISES

6.1. For each of the following groups of query rules, say which rule is best in terms of worst case evaluation complexity using our standard algorithm without indexing.

(a)
```
goal(X,Y,Z) :- p(X,Y) & q(X,X) & r(X,Y,Z)
goal(X,Y,Z) :- p(X,Y) & r(X,Y,Z) & q(X,X)
goal(X,Y,Z) :- q(X,X) & p(X,Y) & r(X,Y,Z)
goal(X,Y,Z) :- q(X,X) & r(X,Y,Z) & p(X,Y)
goal(X,Y,Z) :- r(X,Y,Z) & p(X,Y) & q(X,X)
goal(X,Y,Z) :- r(X,Y,Z) & q(X,X) & p(X,Y)
```

(b)
```
goal(X,Y,Z) :- p(X,Y) & q(a,b) & r(X,Y,Z)
goal(X,Y,Z) :- p(X,Y) & r(X,Y,Z) & q(a,b)
goal(X,Y,Z) :- q(a,b) & p(X,Y) & r(X,Y,Z)
goal(X,Y,Z) :- q(a,b) & r(X,Y,Z) & p(X,Y)
goal(X,Y,Z) :- r(X,Y,Z) & p(X,Y) & q(a,b)
goal(X,Y,Z) :- r(X,Y,Z) & q(a,b) & p(X,Y)
```

(c)
```
goal(X,Y,Z) :- p(X,Y,Z) & q(X) & ~r(X,Y)
goal(X,Y,Z) :- p(X,Y,Z) & ~r(X,Y) & q(X)
goal(X,Y,Z) :- q(X) & p(X,Y,Z) & ~r(X,Y)
goal(X,Y,Z) :- q(X) & ~r(X,Y) & p(X,Y,Z)
goal(X,Y,Z) :- ~r(X,Y) & q(X) & p(X,Y,Z)
goal(X,Y,Z) :- ~r(X,Y) & p(X,Y,Z) & q(X)
```

6.2. For each of the following groups of query rules, select the alternative that is equivalent to the first rule in the group.

(a)
```
goal(X) :- p(X,Y) & q(Y) & q(Z)
goal(X) :- p(X,Y)
goal(X) :- p(X,Y) & q(Y)
goal(X) :- p(X,Y) & q(Z)
```

(b)
```
goal(X) :- p(X) & q(X) & q(W)
goal(X) :- p(X)
goal(X) :- p(X) & q(X)
goal(X) :- p(X) & q(W)
```

(c)
```
goal(X,Y,Z) :- p(X,Y) & q(Y) & q(Z) & q(W)
goal(X,Y,Z) :- p(X,Y) & q(Y) & q(Z)
goal(X,Y,Z) :- p(X,Y) & q(Y) & q(W)
goal(X,Y,Z) :- p(X,Y) & q(Z) & q(W)
```

6.3. For each of the following pairs of queries, say whether the first query subsumes the second, i.e., whether the set of answers to the first query contains the answers to the second query.

(a)
```
goal(X) :- p(X,Y)
goal(X) :- p(X,a) & p(X,b)
```

(b)
```
goal(X) :- p(X,a)
goal(X) :- p(X,Y)
```

(c)
```
goal(X) :- p(X,Y) & p(X,Z)
goal(X) :- p(X,b) & q(b)
```

PART III

View Definitions

CHAPTER 7

View Definitions

7.1 INTRODUCTION

Consider the kinship dataset shown below. The situation here is the same as that described in Chapter 2. Art is the parent of Bob and Bea. Bob is the parent of Cal and Cam. Bea is the parent of Coe and Cory.

```
parent(art,bob)
parent(art,bea)
parent(bob,cal)
parent(bob,cam)
parent(bea,coe)
parent(bea,cory)
```

Suppose now that we wanted to express information about the grandparent relation as well as the parent relation. As illustrated in the preceding chapter, we can do this by adding facts to our dataset. In this case, we would add the facts shown below. Art is the grandparent of Cal and Cam and Coe and Cory.

```
grandparent(art,cal)
grandparent(art,cam)
grandparent(art,coe)
grandparent(art,cory)
```

Unfortunately, doing things this way is wasteful. The grandparent relation can be defined in terms of the parent relation, and so storing grandparent data as well as parent data is redundant.

A better alternative is to write rules to encode such definitions and to use these rules to compute the relations defined by these rules when needed. As we shall see in this chapter, we can write such definitions using rules similar those that we used to define goal relations in Chapter 3. For example, in the case above, rather than adding grandparent facts to our dataset, we can write the following rule, safe in the knowledge that we can use the rule to compute our grandparent data.

```
grandparent(X,Z) :- parent(X,Y) & parent(Y,Z)
```

In what follows, we distinguish two different types of relations—*base relations* and *view relations*. We define base relations by writing facts in a dataset, and we define view relations by writing rules in a *ruleset*. In our example, `parent` is a base relation, and `grandparent` is a view relation.

Given a dataset defining our base relations and a ruleset defining our view relations, we can use automated reasoning tools to derive facts about our view relations. For example, given the preceding facts about the `parent` relation and our rule defining the `grandparent` relation, we can compute the facts about the `grandparent` relation.

Using rules to define view relations has multiple advantages over encoding those relations in the form of datasets. First of all, as we have just seen, there is economy: if view relations are defined in terms of rules, we do not need to store as many facts in our datasets. Second, there is less chance of things getting out of sync, e.g., if we change the parent relation and forget to change the grandparent relation. Third, view definitions work for any number of objects; they even work for applications with infinitely many objects (e.g., the integers) without requiring infinite storage.

In this chapter, we introduce the syntax and semantics of view definitions, and we describe the important notion of stratification. In subsequent chapters, we look at many, many examples of using rules to define views. And, in Chapters 11 and 12, we look at some practical techniques for using rules to compute view relations.

7.2 SYNTAX

The syntax of view definitions is almost identical to that of queries as described in Chapter 3. The various types of constants are the same, and the notions of term and atom and literal are also the same. The main difference comes in the syntax of rules.

As before, a *rule* is an expression consisting of a distinguished atom, called the *head* and a conjunction of zero or more literals, called the *body*. The literals in the body are called *subgoals*. In what follows, we write rules as in the example shown below. Here, `r(X,Y)` is the head; `p(X,Y) & ~q(Y)` is the body; and `p(X,Y)` and `~q(Y)` are subgoals.

```
r(X,Y) :- p(X,Y) & ~q(Y)
```

Despite these similarities, there are two important differences between query rules and rules used in view definitions. (1) In writing query rules, we use a single generic predicate (e.g., `goal`) in the heads of all of our query rules. By contrast, in view definitions, we use predicates for the relations we are defining (e.g., `r` in the example above). (2) In writing query rules, the subgoals of our rules can mention only predicates for relations described in the dataset. By contrast, in view definitions, subgoals can contain view predicates as well as predicates for base relations.

One benefit of the more flexible syntax in view definitions is that we can define multiple relations in a single set of rules. For example, the following rules define both the f relation and the m relation in terms of p and q.

```
f(X,Y) :- p(X,Y) & q(X)
m(X,Y) :- p(X,Y) & ~q(X)
```

A second benefit is that we can use view relations in defining other view relations. For example, in the following rule, we use the view relation f in our definition of g.

```
g(X,Z) :- f(X,Y) & p(Y,Z)
```

A third benefit is that views can be used in their own definitions, thus allowing us to define relations recursively. For example, the following rules define a to be the transitive closure of p.

```
a(X,Z) :- p(X,Z)
a(X,Z) :- p(X,Y) & a(Y,Z)
```

Unfortunately, our relaxed language allows for rulesets with some unpleasant properties. To avoid these problems, it is good practice to comply with some syntactic restrictions on our datasets and rulesets, viz. compatibility and stratification and safety.

A ruleset is *compatible* with a dataset if and only if (1) all symbols shared between the dataset and the ruleset are of the same type (symbol, constructor, predicate), (2) all constructors and predicates have the same arity, and (3) none of the predicates in the dataset appear in the heads of any rules in the ruleset.

7.3 SEMANTICS

The semantics of view definitions is more complicated than the semantics of queries due to the possible occurrence of view predicates in subgoals; and, consequently, we take a slightly different approach.

To define the result of applying a set of view definitions to a dataset, we first combine the facts in a dataset with the rules defining our views into a joint set of facts and rules, hereafter called a *closed logic program*, and we then define the extension of that closed logic program as follows.

The *Herbrand universe* for a closed logic program is the set of all ground terms that can be formed from the symbols and constructors in the program. For a program without constructors, the Herbrand universe is finite (i.e., just the symbols). For a program with constructors, the Herbrand universe is infinite (i.e., the symbols and all compound terms that can be formed from those symbols).

The *Herbrand base* for a closed logic program is the set of all atoms that can be formed from the constants in the program. Said another way, it is the set of all facts of the form $r(t_1,...,t_n)$, where r is an n-ary predicate and $t_1,...,t_n$ are ground terms.

An *interpretation* for a closed logic program is an arbitrary subset of the Herbrand base for the program. As with datasets, the idea here is that the factoids in the interpretation are assumed to be true, and those that are not included are assumed to be false.

A *model* of a closed logic program is an interpretation that *satisfies* the program. We define satisfaction in two steps—we first deal with the case of ground rules, and we then deal with arbitrary rules.

An interpretation Γ satisfies a ground atom ϕ if and only if ϕ is in Γ. Γ satisfies a ground negation ~ϕ if and only if ϕ is *not* in Γ. Γ satisfies a ground rule ϕ :- ϕ_1 & ... & ϕ_n if and only if Γ satisfies ϕ whenever it satisfies $\phi_1,..., \phi_n$.

An *instance* of a rule in a closed logic program is a rule in which all variables have been consistently replaced by terms from the Herbrand universe, i.e., the set of ground terms that can be formed from the program's vocabulary. As before, *consistent replacement* means that, if an occurrence of a variable in a sentence is replaced by a given term, then all occurrences of that variable in that sentence are replaced by the same term.

Using the notion of instance, we can define the notion of satisfaction for arbitrary closed logic programs (with or without variables). An interpretation Γ *satisfies* an arbitrary closed logic program Ω if and only if Γ satisfies every ground instance of every sentence in Ω.

As an example of these concepts, consider the dataset shown below.

```
p(a,b)
p(b,c)
p(c,d)
p(d,c)
```

And let's assume we have the following view definition.

```
r(X,Y) :- p(X,Y) & ~p(Y,X)
```

The following interpretation satisfies the closed logic program consisting of this dataset and ruleset. All of the facts in the dataset are included in the interpretation, and every conclusion that is required by our rule is included as well.

```
p(a,b)
p(b,c)
p(c,d)
p(d,c)
```

```
r(a,b)
r(b,c)
```

By contrast, the following interpretations do *not* satisfy the program. The one on the left is missing conclusions from the rule; the one in the middle is missing the facts from the dataset; and the one on the right satisfies the rules but does not contain all of the facts from the dataset.

```
p(a,b)        r(a,b)        p(a,b)
p(b,c)        r(b,c)        p(b,c)
p(c,d)                      p(c,d)
p(d,c)                      r(a,b)
                            r(b,c)
                            r(c,d)
```

On the other hand, the model shown above (the interpretation before these three non-models) is not the only interpretation that works. In general, a closed logic program can have more than one model, which means that there can be more than one way to satisfy the rules in the program. The following interpretations also satisfy our closed logic program.

```
p(a,b)        p(a,b)        p(a,b)
p(b,c)        p(b,c)        p(b,c)
p(c,d)        p(c,d)        p(c,d)
p(d,c)        p(d,c)        p(d,c)
r(a,b)        r(a,b)        r(a,b)
r(b,c)        r(b,c)        r(b,c)
r(c,d)        r(d,c)        r(c,d)
                            r(d,c)
```

This seems odd in that there is no reason to include `r(c,d)` or `r(d,c)` in our interpretation. On the other hand, given our definition of satisfaction, there is no reason *not* to include them.

The reason that this seems wrong is that we normally want our definitions to be *if and only if*. We want to include among our conclusions only those facts that *must* be true. (1) All factoids in our dataset must be true. (2) All factoids required by our rules must be true. (3) All other factoids should be excluded.

This is the classic definition of what is know as *logical entailment*. A factoid is *logically entailed* by a closed logic program if and only if it is true in every model of the program, i.e., the set of conclusions is the intersection of all models of the program.

One way to ensure logical entailment is to take the intersection of all interpretations that satisfy our program. This guarantees that we get only those conclusions that are true in every model. For example, if we took the intersection of the three models shown above, we would get our original model.

Another approach is to concentrate on *minimal models*. A model Γ of a logic program Ω is *minimal* if and only if there is no proper subset of Γ that is a model for Ω. If there is just one minimal model of a closed logic program, then minimality guarantees logical entailment. For example, the first model given above is minimal, and every factoid in that model must be present in every model of the program.

Many closed logic programs have unique minimal models. For example, a closed logic program that does not contain any negations has one and only one minimal model. Unfortunately, closed logic programs with negation can have more than one minimal model.

One way of eliminating with ambiguities like this is to concentrate on programs that are *semipositive* or programs that are *stratified* with respect to negation. We define these types of programs and discuss their semantics in the next two sections.

7.4 SEMIPOSITIVE PROGRAMS

A semipositive program is one in which negations apply only to base relations, i.e., there are no subgoals with negated views.

The semantics of a semipositive program can be formalized by defining the result of applying the view definitions in the program to the facts in the program's dataset. We use the word *extension* to refer to the set of all facts that can be "deduced" in this way.

An *instance* of an expression (atom, literal, or rule) is one in which all variables have been consistently replaced by ground terms. For example, if we have a language with object constants `a` and `b`, then `r(a) :- p(a,a)`, `r(a) :- p(a,b)`, `r(b) :- p(b,a)`, and `r(b) :- p(b,b)` are all instances of `r(X) :- p(X,Y)`.

Given this notion, we define the result of the application of a single rule to a dataset as follows. Given a rule r and a dataset Δ, let $v(r,\Delta)$ be the set of all ψ such that (1) ψ is the head of an arbitrary instance of r, (2) every positive subgoal in the instance is a member of Δ, and (3) no negative subgoal in the instance is a member of Δ.

Using this notion, we define the result of repeatedly applying a *single stratum* of rules Ω to a dataset Δ as follows. Consider the sequence of datasets defined recursively as follows. $\Gamma_0 = \Delta$, and $\Gamma_{n+1} = \cap v(r,\Gamma_0 \cap ... \cap \Gamma_n)$ for all r in Ω. The closure of Ω on Δ is the union of the datasets in this sequence, i.e., $C(\Omega,\Delta) = \cap \Gamma_i$.

To illustrate our definition, let's start with a dataset describing a small directed graph. In the sentences below, we use the `edge` predicate to record the arcs of one particular graph.

```
edge(a,b)
edge(b,c)
```

```
edge(c,d)
edge(d,c)
```

Now, let's write some rules defining various relations on the nodes in our graph. Here, the relation p is true of nodes with an outgoing arc. The relation q is true of two nodes if and only if there is an edge from the first to the second *or* an edge from the second to the first. The relation r is true of two nodes if and only if there is an edge from the first to the second *and* an edge from the second to the first. The relation s is the transitive closure of the edge relation.

```
p(X) :- edge(X,Y)
q(X,Y) :- edge(X,Y)
q(X,Y) :- edge(Y,X)
r(X,Y,Z) :- edge(X,Y) & edge(Y,Z)
s(X,Y) :- edge(X,Y)
s(X,Z) :- edge(X,Y) & s(Y,Z)
```

We start the computation by initializing our dataset to the edge facts listed above.

```
edge(a,b)
edge(b,c)
edge(c,d)
edge(d,c)
```

Looking at the p rule and matching its subgoals to the data in our dataset in all possible ways, we see that we can add the following facts. In this case, every node in our graph has an outgoing edge, so there is one p fact for each node.

```
p(a)
p(b)
p(c)
p(d)
```

Looking at the q rules and matching their subgoals to the data in our dataset in all possible ways, we see that we can add the following facts. In this case, we end up with the symmetric closure of the original graph.

```
q(a,b)
q(b,a)
q(b,c)
```

```
q(c,b)
q(c,d)
q(d,c)
```

Looking at the r rule and matching the subgoals to the data in our dataset in all possible ways, we see that we can add the following facts.

```
r(c,d)
r(d,c)
```

Finally, looking at the first rule for s and matching its subgoals to the data in our dataset in all possible ways, we see that we can add the following facts.

```
s(a,b)
s(b,c)
s(c,d)
s(d,c)
```

However, we are not quite done. With the facts just added, we can use the second rule to derive the following additional data.

```
s(a,c)
s(b,d)
s(c,c)
s(d,d)
```

Having done this, we can use the s rule again and can derive the following fact.

```
s(a,d)
```

At this point, none of the rules when applied to this collection of data produces any results that are not already in the set, and so the process terminates. The resulting collection of 25 facts is the extension of this program.

7.5 STRATIFIED PROGRAMS

We say that a set of view definitions is *stratified* if and only if its rules can be partitioned into *strata* in such a way that (1) every stratum contains at least one rule, (2) the rules defining relations that appear in positive subgoals of a rule appear in the same stratum as that rule *or* in some lower stratum, and (3) the rules defining relations that appear in negative subgoals of a rule occur in some *lower* stratum (not the same stratum).

As an example, assume we have a unary relation p that is true of all of the objects in some application area, and assume that q is an arbitrary binary relation. Now, consider the ruleset shown below. The first two rules define r to be the transitive closure of q. The third rule defines s to be the complement of the transitive closure.

```
r(X,Y) :- q(X,Y)
r(X,Z) :- q(X,Y) & r(Y,Z)
s(X,Y) :- p(X) & p(Y) & ~r(X,Y)
```

This is a complicated ruleset, yet it is easy to see that it is stratified. The first two rules contain no negations at all, and so we can group them together in our lowest stratum. The third rule has a negated subgoal containing a relation defined in our lowest stratum, and so we put it into a stratum above this one, as shown below. This ruleset satisfies the conditions of our definition and hence it is stratified.

Stratum	Rules
2	s(X,Y) :- p(X) & p(Y) & ~r(X,Y)
1	r(X,Y) :- q(X,Y)
	r(X,Z) :- q(X,Y) & r(Y,Z)

By comparison, consider the following ruleset. Here, the relation r is defined in terms of p and q, and the relation s is defined in terms of r and the negation of s.

```
r(X,Y) :- p(X) & p(Y) & q(X,Y)
s(X,Y) :- r(X,Y) & ~s(Y,X)
```

There is no way of dividing the rules of this ruleset into strata in a way that satisfies the definition above. Hence, the ruleset is *not* stratified.

The problem with unstratified rulesets is that there is a potential ambiguity. As an example, consider the rules above and assume that our dataset also included the facts p(a), p(b), q(a,b), and q(b,a). From these facts, we can conclude r(a,b) and r(b,a) are both true. So far, so good. But what can we say about s? If we take s(a,b) to be true and s(b,a) to be false, then the second rule is satisfied. If we take s(a,b) to be false and s(b,a) to be true, then the second rule is again satisfied. The upshot is that there is ambiguity about s. By concentrating exclusively on logic programs that are stratified, we avoid such ambiguities.

Although it is sometimes possible to stratify the rules in more than one way, this does not cause any problems. So long as a program is stratified with respect to negation, the definition just given produces the same extension no matter which stratification one uses.

Finally, we define the *extension* of a ruleset Ω on dataset Δ as follows. The definition relies on a decomposition of Ω into strata $\Omega_1,...,\Omega_k$. Since there are only finitely many rules in a closed logic program and every stratum must contain at least one rule, there are only finitely many sets to consider (though the sets themselves might be infinite). With that in mind, let $\Delta_0 = \Delta$, and let $\Delta_{n+1} = \Delta_n \cap C(\Omega_{n+1},\Delta_n)$. The extension of a program with k strata is just Δ_k.

The extension of any closed logic program without constructors must be finite. Also, the extension of any non-recursive closed logic program must be finite. In both cases, it is possible to compute the extension in finite time. In fact, it is possible to show that the computation cost is polynomial in the size of the dataset.

In the case of recursive programs without constructors, the result must still be finite. However, the cost of computing the extension may be exponential in the size of the data, but the result can be computed in finite time.

For recursive programs with constructors, it is possible that the extension is infinite. In such cases, the extension is still well-defined; and, although we obviously cannot generate the entire extension in finite time, if a factoid is in the extension, it is possible to.

The preceding section illustrates our method of computing extensions for semipositive programs. We now extend our example to show how to compute the extension of a stratified program.

Suppose we add the rule shown below to the program in the preceding section. The relation `t` here is the complement of the transitive closure of the `edge` relation.

```
t(X,Y) :- p(X) & p(Y) & ~s(X,Y)
```

Since this rule contains a negated relation, it would necessarily appear at a higher stratum than the `s` relation, and so we would not compute the conclusions until after we were done with `s`.

In this case, there are sixteen ways to satisfy the first two subgoals of our rule; and, as we saw in the preceding section, nine of them satisfy the `s` relation. The upshot is that the remaining seven facts satisfy the `t` relation. So, we can add these to our extension.

```
s(a,a)
s(b,a)
s(b,b)
s(c,a)
s(c,b)
s(d,a)
s(d,b)
```

Note that, in the presence of rules with negated subgoals, it is sometimes possible to stratify the rules in more than one way. The good news here is that does not cause any problems.

So long as a program is stratified with respect to negation, the definition just given produces the same dataset no matter which stratification one uses. Consequently, there is just one extension for any safe, stratified logic program.

7.6 EXERCISES

7.1. Say whether each of the following expressions is a syntactically legal view definition.

(a) `r(X,Y) :- p(X,Y) & q()`
(b) `r(X,Y) :- p(X,Y) & ~q(Y,X)`
(c) `~r(X,Y) :- p(X,Y) & q(Y,X)`
(d) `p(X,Y) & q(Y,X) :- r(X,Y)`
(e) `p(X,Y) & ~q(Y,X) :- r(X,Y)`

7.2. Suppose we have a dataset with two symbols `a` and `b` and two unary relations `p` and `q` where all possible facts are true, i.e., the dataset is {`p(a)`, `p(b)`, `q(a)`, `q(b)`}. Suppose we have a closed logic program consisting of this dataset and the rule `r(X) :- p(X) & ~q(X)`.

(a) How many interpretations does this program have?
(b) How many models does it have?
(c) How many minimal models does it have?

7.3. Say whether each of the following rulesets is stratified.

(a)
```
r(X,Y) :- p(X,Y) & ~q(Y,X)
r(X,Y) :- p(X,Y) & ~q(X,Y)
```

(b)
```
r(X,Z) :- p(X,Z) & q(X,Z)
r(X,Z) :- r(X,Y) & ~r(Y,Z)
```

(c)
```
r(X,Z) :- p(X,Z) & ~q(X,Z)
r(X,Z) :- r(X,Y) & r(Y,Z)
```

7.4. What is $v(r,\Delta)$ where r is `r(X,Y) :- p(X,Y) & p(Y,X)` and Δ is the dataset shown below?

```
p(a,a)
p(a,b)
p(b,a)
p(b,c)
```

7.5. What is C(Ω,Δ) where Ω is {`r(X,Z) :- p(X,Z)`,`r(X,Z) :- r(X,Y) & r(Y,Z)`} and Δ is the dataset shown below?

```
p(a,a)
p(a,b)
p(b,a)
p(b,c)
```

7.6. What is the extension of strata Ω_1 and Ω_2 on Δ, where Ω_1 is {`q(X) :- p(X,Y)`}, where Ω_2 is {`r(X,Y) :- p(X,Y) & ~q(Y)`}, and where Δ is the dataset shown below?

```
p(a,b)
p(a,c)
p(b,d)
p(c,d)
```

CHAPTER 8

View Evaluation

8.1 INTRODUCTION

In the preceding chapter, we defined the result of applying a stratified logic program to a dataset in a constructive manner—starting with the dataset and successively applying the program's strata to produce an extension of the program as a whole. This definition readily translates to a practical method of computing such extensions known as *bottom-up* evaluation.

Although bottom-up evaluation is used in some Logic Programming systems, many evaluation engines use a *top-down* approach to answering questions. Instead of starting with data and working upward, such engines start with a query to be answered and work downward, using rules to reduce the goals to subgoals until they reach subgoals written entirely in terms of base relations.

The benefit of doing things this way is that such evaluation engines avoid the generation of large numbers of conclusions that have nothing to do with the question at hand. More significantly, in cases where there are infinitely many possible conclusions, they can often find answers to specific questions without doing infinitely much work.

One downside to top-down evaluation is that, for some people, it is more difficult to understand than bottom-up evaluation. There is also a danger of unnecessary infinite loops if rules are written badly. However, that danger can be minimized or eliminated by understanding how the procedure works. A little familiarity with top-down processing can help one understand how it works and can help one avoid writing bad rules.

In this chapter, we introduce a particular top-down evaluation procedure. We begin by defining a top-down, backtracking approach to processing goals and rules without variables. We then introduce the key process of unification. Finally, we put the two together in a top-down procedure for arbitrary goals and rules.

8.2 TOP-DOWN PROCESSING OF GROUND GOALS AND RULES

In this section, we begin our discussion of top-down evaluation by focussing on goals and rules without variables. In the next section, we look at a way of comparing expressions containing variables. In the section after that, we show how to combine that technique with the procedure described here to produce an evaluation procedure for arbitrary goals and rules.

Top-down evaluation is a recursive procedure. We start with a goal to be "proved." We either prove the goal directly or we reduce it to one or more subgoals and try to prove those subgoals. The way we process a goal depends on the type of the goal we are given.

1. If the goal is an atom and the predicate in the goal is a base relation, we simply check whether the goal is contained in our dataset. If it is there, we succeed. If not, we fail.

2. If the goal is a negative literal, we execute the procedure on the argument of the negation. If we succeed in proving the argument, then the negation as a whole is false, and the procedure fails. If we *fail* to prove the argument, then the negation as a whole is true, and so we succeed.

3. If our goal is a conjunction of literals, we first execute our procedure on the first conjunct. If we succeed in proving that goal, we move on to the next conjunct and so forth until we are done. If we fail to prove any one of the goals, then we fail to prove the conjunction as a whole.

4. If the goal is an atom and the predicate in the goal is a view relation, we examine all rules with our goal as head. For each such rule, we execute our procedure on the body of the rule. We succeed on our goal if and only if we can succeed on the body of some rule; otherwise, we fail.

As an example, consider the dataset shown on the left below and the rule set shown on the right. There are three base relations – p, q, r; and there are two view relations – s and t.

```
p(a)              s(b) :- p(a) & q(b) & r(c)
q(a)              s(b) :- p(a) & ~q(b) & ~t(c)
r(a)              t(c) :- r(c)
                  t(c) :- r(d)
```

Now, imagine that we are asked whether to evaluate the goal `s(b)`. Since `s` is a view relation, we examine the rules containing `s(b)` in the head and execute the procedure on the bodies of these rules, one after another until we find one that succeeds.

Using the first rule for `s(b)`, we reduce our goal to the conjunction `(p(a) & q(b) & r(c))` and evaluate this subgoal. Since `p` is a base relation, we simply check our dataset for the literal `p(a)`. Since `p(a)` is in the dataset, that subgoal evaluates to true and we move on to the second conjunct `q(b)`. Since `q` is a base relation, again we check our dataset for the literal `q(b)`. Unfortunately, in this case, we fail since `q(b)` is not a member of the dataset. At this point, we terminate processing of the conjunction. (Since the conjunction as a whole is false, there is no point in check `r(c)`.)

Having failed to prove the body of the first rule, we move on to the second rule and try again, this time with `p(a) & ~q(b) & ~t(c)` as our goal. As before, we find that `p(a)` is true and we move on to the second conjunct. In this case, we have a negation, so we execute the procedure recursively on `q(b)`. As before, we fail. Therefore, the subgoal `~q(b)` is true. The upshot is that this time we continue and execute the procedure on `~t(c)`. Since `t` is view relation, we execute the procedure on the bodies of the rules containing `t(c)` in the head. In this case, we first try `r(c)` and fail; then we try `r(d)` and fail once again. Having exhausted all of the rules defining `t(c)`, we fail to prove `t(c)`. This means that the negation `~t(c)` is true. The upshot of that is that the conjunction `(p(a) & ~q(b) & ~t(c))` is true; and, hence, our overall goal `s(b)` is true.

8.3 UNIFICATION

Unifcation is the process of determining whether two expressions can be *unified*, i.e., made identical by appropriate substitutions for their variables. As we shall see, making this determination is an essential part of top-down evaluation.

A *substitution* is a finite mapping of variables to terms. In what follows, we write substitutions as sets of replacement rules, like the one shown below. In each rule, the variable to which the arrow is pointing is to be replaced by the term from which the arrow is pointing. In this case, `X` is to be replaced by `a`, `Y` is to be replaced by `f(b)`, and `Z` is to be replaced by `V`.

```
{X←a, Y←f(b), Z←V}
```

The variables being replaced together constitute the *domain* of the substitution, and the terms replacing them constitute the *range*. For example, in the preceding substitution, the domain is {X, Y, Z}, and the range is {a, f(b), V}.

The result of applying a substitution σ to an expression ϕ is the expression $\phi\sigma$ obtained from the original expression by replacing every occurrence of every variable in the domain of the substitution by the term with which it is associated.

```
q(X,Y){X←a, Y←f(b), Z←V} = q(a,f(b))
q(X,X){X←a, Y←f(b), Z←V} = q(a,a)
q(X,W){X←a, Y←f(b), Z←V} = q(a, W)
q(Z,V){X←a, Y←f(b), Z←V} = q(V,V)
```

Given two or more substitutions, it is possible to define a single substitution that has the same effect as applying those substitutions in sequence. For example, the substitutions {X←a, Y←U, Z←V} and {U←d, V←e} can be combined to form the single substitution {X←a, Y←d, Z←e, U←d, V←e}, which has the same effect as the first two substitutions when applied to any expression whatsoever.

Computing the *composition* of a substitution σ and a substitution τ is easy. There are two steps. (1) First, we apply τ to the range of σ. (2) Then we adjoin to σ all pairs from τ with different domain variables.

As an example, consider the composition shown below. In the right-hand side of the first equation, we have applied the second substitution to the replacements in the first substitution.

In the second equation, we have combined the rules from this new substitution with the non-conflicting rules from the second substitution.

{X←a, Y←U, Z←V}{U←d, V←e, Z←g}
= {X←a, Y←d, Z←e}{U←d, V←e, Z←g}
= {X←a, Y←d, Z←e, U←d, V←e}

A substitution σ is a *unifier* for an expression ϕ and an expression ψ if and only if $\phi\sigma=\psi\sigma$, i.e., the result of applying σ to ϕ is the same as the result of applying σ to ψ. If two expressions have a unifier, they are said to be *unifiable.*

The expressions p(X,Y) and p(a,V) have a unifier, e.g., {X←a, Y←b, V←b} and are, therefore, unifiable. The results of applying this substitution to the two expressions are shown below.

p(X,Y){X←a, Y← b, V←b} = p(a,b)
p(a,V){X←a, Y← b, V←b} = p(a,b)

Note that, although this substitution is a unifier for the two expressions, it is not the only unifier. We do not have to substitute b for Y and V to unify the two expressions. We can equally well substitute c or f(c) or f(W). In fact, we can unify the expressions without changing V at all by simply replacing Y by V.

In considering these alternatives, it should be clear that some substitutions are more general than others. We say that a substitution σ is *as general as or more general than* a substitution τ if and only if there is another substitution δ such that $\sigma\delta=\tau$. For example, the substitution {X←a, Y←V} is more general than {X←a, Y←c, V←b} since there is a substitution {V←c} that, when applied to the former, gives the latter.

{X←a, Y←V}{V←c}={X←a, Y←c, V←c}

In top-down evaluation, we are interested only in unifiers with maximum generality. A *most general unifier* σ of two expressions has the property that it is general as or more general than any other unifier.

Although it is possible for two expressions to have more than one most general unifier, all of these most general unifiers are structurally the same, i.e., they are unique up to variable renaming. For example, p(X) and p(Y) can be unified by either the substitution {X←Y} or the substitution {Y←X}; and either of these substitutions can be obtained from the other by applying a third substitution. This is not true of the substitutions mentioned earlier.

One good thing about our language is that there is a simple and inexpensive procedure for computing a most general unifier of any two expressions if it exists.

The procedure assumes a representation of expressions as sequences of subexpressions. For example, the expression p(a,b,Z) can be thought of as a sequence with four elements, viz. the predicate p, the symbol a, the symbol b, and the variable Z.

The procedure also assumes that the two expressions have no variables in common. As we shall see in the next section, we can assure this by renaming the variables in one of the expressions.

We start the procedure with two expressions and a substitution, which is initially the empty substitution. We then recursively process the two expressions, comparing the subexpressions at each point. Along the way, we expand the substitution with variable assignments as described below. If, we fail to unify any pair of subexpression at any point in this process, the procedure as a whole fails. If we finish this recursive comparison of the expressions, the procedure as a whole succeeds, and the accumulated substitution at that point is the most general unifier.

In comparing two subexpressions, we first apply the substitution to each of the two expressions; and we then execute the following procedure on the two modified expressions.

1. If one expression is a symbol and the other expression is the same symbol, then the procedure succeeds, returning the unmodified substitution as result.

2. If one expression is a symbol and the other expression is a different symbol or a compound expression, then the procedure fails.

3. If one expression is a variable and the other expression is the same variable, then the procedure succeeds, returning the unmodified substitution as result.

4. If at least one expression is a variable and the other expression is any other expression, we proceed as follows. First, we check whether the other expression contains the variable. If the variable occurs within the other expression, we fail (for reasons described below). Otherwise, we update our substitution to the composition of the old substitution and a new substitution in which we bind the variable to the second modified expression.

5. If the two expressions are sequences of the same length, we iterate across the expressions, comparing as described above.

6. If the expressions are compound expressions of a different length, the procedure fails.

As an example of this procedure in operation, consider the computation of the most general unifier for the expressions `p(X,b)` and `p(a,Y)` with the initial substitution {}. A trace of the execution of the procedure for this case is shown below. We show the beginning of a comparison with a line labeled "Compare" together with the expressions being compared and the input substitution. We show the result of each comparison with a line labeled "Result" (either a substitution where successful or "false" where unsuccessful). The indentation shows the depth of recursion of the procedure.

Compare: p(X,b), p(a,Y), {}

Compare: p, p, {}

Result: {}

Compare: X, a, {}

Result: {X←a}

Compare: Y, b, {X←a}

Result: {X←a, Y← b}

Result: {x←a, y←b}

As another example, consider the process of unifying the expression p(X,X) and the expression p(a,Y). A trace is shown below. The main interest in this example comes in comparing the last argument in the two expressions, viz. X and Y. By the time we reach this point, X is bound to a, so we call the procedure recursively on a and Y, which results in a binding of Y to a.

Compare: p(X,X), p(a,Y), {}

Compare: p, p, {}

Result: {}

Compare: X, a, {}

Result: {X←a}

Compare: X, Y, {X←a}

Compare: a, Y, {X← a}

Result: {X←a, Y← a}

Result: {X←a, Y← a}

Result: {X←a, Y←a}

One noteworthy part of the unification procedure is the test for whether a variable occurs within an expression before the variable is bound to that expression. This test is called an *occur check* since it is used to check whether or not the variable occurs within the term with which it is being unified. For example, in trying to unify p(X,X) and p(Y,f(Y)), we would not want to bind Y to f(Y), since these expressions can never be made to look alike by substituting and value for Y *consistently* throughout the expression.

8.4 TOP-DOWN PROCESSING OF NON-GROUND QUERIES AND RULES

Using unification, we can convert our procedure for top-down evaluation for ground queries and rules to a procedure for evaluating arbitrary queries and rules. There are three salient changes. (1) The procedure is begun with a goal *and* a substitution. (2) Rather than checking whether a goal and a factoid or a rule head are identical, the procedure checks whether or not they are unifiable. (3) Instead of returning a Boolean value from each recursive call, the procedure returns a substitution that makes the given goal true and it uses this substitution in processing any remaining subgoals. The steps of the procedure are described below.

1. If the predicate in the goal is a base relation, we iterate through our dataset comparing the goal to each factoid in turn. If there is an extension of the given substitution that unifies the goal and the factoid, we add that extended substitution to our list of answers. Once we have finished examining all relevant factoids, we return the list of substitutions we have accumulated along the way. (If we do not find any factoids that unify with the goal, we return an empty list.)

2. If our goal is a negative literal, we execute the procedure on the argument of the negation and the given substitution. If the result is empty, we return a singleton list containing the given substitution. Otherwise, we return the empty list, indicating failure to prove the negation.

3. If our goal is a conjunction of literals, we first execute our procedure on the first conjunct and the given substitution to get a list of substitutions that satisfy that conjunct. We then iterate through the list of substitutions, calling the procedure recursively on the remaining conjuncts with each substitution in turn. We collect the answers from these recursive calls. We return the list of these answers as value of the procedure.

4. If our goal is an atom and the predicate is a view relation, we iterate through the rules in our program. We first copy each rule, replacing the variables by new variables (to avoid possible conflicts with variables in our goal). We then try to find a most general unifier for the given goal and the head of the rule starting with the given substitution. If we succeed, we call the procedure recursively on the body of the rule and the resulting unifier. We add all substitutions returned from this recursive call to our output list. When we have finished examining all of the rules, we return the substitutions we have collected along the way.

Once again, consider the dataset we saw earlier (repeated on the left below), and consider a version of the logic program with some of the object constants replaced by variables (shown on the right below).

```
p(a)            s(X) :- t(X) & ~r(X)
p(b)            s(X) :- p(X) & ~q(X) & ~t(c)
p(c)            t(X) :- p(X) & q(X)
q(b)            t(X) :- r(X)
r(c)
```

To see our procedure in action, let's start with a simple case. Imagine that we want to find all objects that appear in both the p relation and the q relation. We call our procedure with p(X) & q(X) as goal and the empty substitution {} as initial substitution. Since our goal is a conjunction, we first call the procedure recursively on p(X) and {}. Our goal p(X) with initial substitution {} unifies all three of the p factoids in our dataset, and so the result of the recursive call is a list of the resulting substitutions, i.e., {X←a} and {X←b} and {X←c}. For each of these substitutions, we then call the procedure recursively on the second conjunct q(X). There is no factoid that unifies with q(X) given the {X←a} substitution, so in this case we return the empty list. In the second case, we are luckier. q(X) and q(b) do unify given the substitution {X←b}, so we return a list containing that substitution. The third case is similar to the first in that there is no unifiable factoid, so again we get an empty list. Having checked the second conjunct for each of the answers to the first conjunct, we return the list of substitutions we have accumulated along the way, in this case the list consisting of the single substitution {X←b}.

As a more interesting example, imagine that we want to evaluate the goal s(X), i.e., we want all objects that satisfy the s relation. We call our procedure with s(X) and the empty substitution {}. Since s is a view relation, we examine the rules where s appears in the head. We copy the first rule resulting in the new rule s(X1) :- p(X1) & q(X1) & r(c), and we try to unify our goal with the head of this rule. In this case, we succeed with the substitution {X←X1}. We then call the procedure recursively on the body of the rule and this substitution and proceed as before, resulting in a final answer containing the single substitution {X←X1, X1←b}.

The procedure just described computes all answers to a given query. If we want just a few answers, we can use a "pipelined" version of the algorithm that returns one answer at a time. When processing a rule, rather than computing all answers to a subgoal before proceeding, once we have a single answer we check whether that solution leads to an answer to the remaining subgoals. If it does, we return that answer. If not, we generate another answer to our subgoal and try again.

8.5 EXERCISES

8.1. Suppose we were to run our top-down evaluation method on the dataset shown below and the ruleset shown on the right. How many dataset accesses would be required to evaluate s(b). (Each time a factoid is looked up counts as one access.)

```
p(a)        s(b) :- p(a) & q(b) & r(c)
q(a)        s(b) :- p(a) & ~q(b) & ~t(c)
r(a)        t(c) :- r(c)
            t(c) :- r(d)
```

8.2. For each of the following pairs of sentences, say whether the sentences are unifiable and give a most general unifier for those that are unifiable.

(a) `p(X,X)` and `p(a,Y)`

(b) `p(X,X)` and `p(f(Y),Z)`

(c) `p(X,X)` and `p(f(Y),Y)`

(d) `p(f(X,Y),g(Z,Z))` and `p(f(f(W,Z),V),W)`

8.3. Suppose we were to run our top-down evaluation method on the dataset shown below and the ruleset shown on the right with the goal `r(a,d)`. Show a trace of subgoals in the order in which they are processed and the results.

```
p(a,b)            r(X,Z) :- p(X,Z)
p(a,c)            r(X,Z) :- p(X,Y) & p(Y,Z)
p(c,d)
```

CHAPTER 9

Examples

9.1 INTRODUCTION

In this chapter, we look at some simple examples of view definitions. The examples here are simple in that do not involve constructors or compound terms. In the following chapters, we look at more complicated examples where constructors and compound terms play an essential role.

9.2 EXAMPLE – KINSHIP

To illustrate the use of rules in defining views, consider once again the world of kinship relations. Starting with some base relations, we can define various interesting view relations.

For example, the first sentence below defines the `father` relation in terms of `parent` and `male`. The second sentence defines `mother` in terms of `parent` and `female`.

```
father(X,Y) :- parent(X,Y) & male(X)
mother(X,Y) :- parent(X,Y) & female(X)
```

The rule below defines the grandparent relation in terms of the parent relation. A person `X` is the grandparent of a person `Z` if `X` is the parent of a person `Y` and `Y` is the parent of `Z`. The variable `Y` here is a *thread variable* that connects the first subgoal to the second but does not itself appear in the head of the rule.

```
grandparent(X,Z) :- parent(X,Y) & parent(Y,Z)
```

Note that the same relation can appear in the head of more than one rule. For example, the `person` relation is true of a person `Y` if there is an `X` such that `X` is the parent of `Y` *or* if `Y` is the parent of some person `Z`. Note that in this case the conditions are disjunctive (at least one must be true), whereas the conditions in the grandfather case are conjunctive (both must be true).

```
person(X) :- parent(X,Y)
person(Y) :- parent(X,Y)
```

A person `X` is an ancestor of a person `Z` if `X` is the parent of `Z` or if there is a person `Y` such that `X` is a parent of `Y` and `Y` is an ancestor of `Z`. This example shows that it is possible for a relation to appear in its own definition. (See below for a discussion of stratification for a restriction on this capability.)

```
ancestor(X,Y) :- parent(X,Y)
ancestor(X,Z) :- parent(X,Y) & ancestor(Y,Z)
```

A person is a parent if and only if the person has children, and a childless person is one who has no children. We can define these properties with the rules shown below. The first rule says that `isparent` is true of `X` if `X` is the parent of some person `Y`. The second rule states that a person `X` is childless if `X` is a person and it is not the case that `X` is a parent.

```
isparent(X) :- parent(X,Y)
childless(X) :- person(X) & ~isparent(X)
```

Note the use of the relation `isparent` in defining `childless`. It is tempting to write the childless rule as `childless(X) :- person(X) & ~parent(X,Y)`. However, this would be wrong. This would define `X` to be childless if `X` is a person and there is *some* `Y` such that `X` is `~parent(X,Y)` is true. But we really want to say that `~parent(X,Y)` holds for *all* `Y`. Defining `isparent` and using its negation in the definition of `childless` allows us to express this *universal quantification*.

9.3 EXAMPLE – BLOCKS WORLD

Once again, consider the Blocks World introduced in Chapter 2. The Blocks World scene described earlier is repeated below (Figure 9.1).

Figure 9.1: One state of Blocks World.

As before, we adopt a vocabulary with five symbols to denote the five blocks in the scene—`a`, `b`, `c`, `d`, and `e`. We use the unary predicate `block` to state that an object is a block. We use the binary predicate `on` to express the fact that one block is directly on another. We use `above` to say that a block is somewhere above another block. We use the unary predicate `cluttered` to a block has other blocks on top of it, and we use the unary predicate `clear` to say that a block has nothing on top of it. We use the unary predicate `supported` to say that a block is resting on another block, and we use the unary predicate `table` to say that a block is resting on the table.

Given this vocabulary, we can describe the scene in Figure 9.1 by writing ground atomic sentences that state which relations hold of which objects or groups of objects. Let's start with `block`. There are five blocks in this case, named `a`, `b`, `c`, `d`, and `e`.

```
block(a)
block(b)
block(c)
block(d)
block(e)
```

Some of these blocks are on top of each other, and some are not. The following sentences capture the relationships in Figure 9.1.

```
on(a,b)
on(b,c)
on(d,e)
```

We can do the same for the other relations. However, there is an easier way. Each of the remaining relations can be defined in terms of `block` and `on`. These definitions together with our facts about the `block` and on relations logically entail every other ground relational sentence or its negation. Hence, given these definitions, we do not need to write out any additional data.

A block satisfies the `cluttered` relation if and only if there is a block resting on it. A block satisfies the `clear` relation if and only if there is nothing on it.

```
cluttered(Y) :- on(X,Y)
clear(X) :- block(X) & ~cluttered(X)
```

A block satisfies the `supported` relation if and only if it is resting on some block. A block satisfies the `table` relation if and only if it is *not* resting on some block.

```
supported(X) :- on(X,Y)
table(X) :- block(X) & ~supported(X)
```

Three blocks satisfy the `stack` relation if and only if the first is on the second and the second is on the third.

```
stack(X,Y,Z) :- on(X,Y) & on(Y,Z)
```

The `above` relation is a bit tricky to define correctly. One block is above another block if and only if the first block is on the second block or it it is on another block that is above the second block. Given a complete definition for the on relation, these two rules determine a unique above relation.

```
above(X,Y) :- on(X,Y)
above(X,Z) :- on(X,Y) & above(Y,Z)
```

One advantage to defining relations in terms of other relations is economy. If we record on information for every object and encode the relationship between the on relation and these other relations, there is no need to record any ground relational sentences for those relations.

Another advantage is that these general sentences apply to Blocks World scenes other than the one pictured here. It is possible to create a Blocks World scene in which none of the on sentences we have listed is true, but these general definitions are still correct.

9.4 EXAMPLE – MODULAR ARITHMETIC

In this example, we show how to define Modular Arithmetic. In Modular Arithmetic, there are only finitely many numbers. For example, in Modular Arithmetic with modulus 4, we have just four integers—0, 1, 2, 3—and that's all. Our goal here is to define addition. Admittedly, this is a modest goal; but, once we see how to do this; we can use the same approach to define other arithmetic concepts.

Let's start with the *number* relation, which is true of every number. We can completely characterize the number relation by writing ground relational sentences, one sentence for each number.

```
number(0)
number(1)
number(2)
number(3)
```

Now, let's define the next relation, which, for each number, gives the next larger number, wrapping back to 0 after we reach 3.

```
next(0,1)
next(1,2)
next(2,3)
next(3,0)
```

The addition table for Modular Arithmetic is the usual addition table for arbitrary numbers except that we wrap around whenever we get past 3. For such a small arithmetic, it is easy to write out the ground facts for addition, as shown below.

```
add(0,0,0)     add(1,0,1)     add(2,0,2)     add(3,0,3)
add(0,1,1)     add(1,1,2)     add(2,1,3)     add(3,1,0)
add(0,2,2)     add(1,2,3)     add(2,2,0)     add(3,2,1)
add(0,3,3)     add(1,3,0)     add(2,3,1)     add(3,3,2)
```

That's one way to do things, but we can do better. Rather than writing out all of those facts, we can use rules to define add in terms of number and next and use those rules to facts about add. The relevant rules are shown below.

```
add(0,Y,Y) :- number(Y)
add(X2,Y,Z2) :- next(X,X2) & distinct(X2,0) & add(X,Y,Z) & next(Z,Z2)
```

First, we have an identity rule. Adding 0 to any number results in the same number. Second we have a successor rule. If X2 is the successor of X and Z is the sum of X and Y and Z2 is the successor of Z, then Z2 is the sum of X2 and Y.

As mentioned earlier, one advantage of doing things this way is economy. With these sentences, we do not need to write out the facts about add given above. They can all be computed from by the facts about next and the rules defining add. A second advantage is versatility. Our sentences define add in terms of next for arithmetic with any modulus, not just modulus 4.

9.5 EXAMPLE – DIRECTED GRAPHS

Consider the problem of describing finite graphs and defining properties of those graphs. Let's start by describing a small directed graph. We use symbols to refer to the nodes of the graph; and we use the edge relation to designate the arcs of the graph. For example, the dataset below describes a graph with 4 nodes and 4 arcs—an arc from a to b, an arc from b to c, an arc from c to d, and an arc from d to c.

```
node(a)
node(b)
node(c)
node(d)

edge(a,b)
edge(b,c)
edge(c,d)
edge(d,c)
```

Now, let's augment this program with some rules defining various relations on the nodes in our graph.

```
p(X) :- edge(X,X)
q(X,Y) :- edge(X,Y)
q(X,Y) :- edge(Y,X)
r(X,Y,Z) :- edge(X,Y) & edge(Y,Z)
s(X,Y) :- edge(X,Y)
s(X,Z) :- edge(X,Y) & s(Y,Z)
```

Here, the relation `p` is true of every node that has an arc to itself. The relation `q` is true of two nodes if and only if there is an edge from the first to the second or from the second to the first. The relation `r` is true of three nodes if and only if there is an edge from the first to the second and an edge from the second to the third. The relation `s` is the transitive closure of the `edge` relation.

Defining properties of a graph as a whole is often tricker than defining properties of individual nodes since we must usually ensure that the properties apply to all of the nodes in the graph. The trick in such situations is to characterize those cases when the graph does *not* have the desired property and then define the desired property as the negation of those cases.

Suppose, for example, we wanted to define the concept of reflexivity. A graph is *reflexive* if and only if every node has an arc to itself. To define this notion, we would first define what it means for a graph to be non-reflexive. A graph is *non-reflexive* if and only if there is a node that does not have a self-arc. Given this definition, we can then define reflexivity as the negation of this property.

```
nonreflexive :- node(X) & ~edge(X,X)
reflexive :- ~nonreflexive
```

We could also define this notion using the `countofall` aggregate as shown below. A graph is *non-reflexive* if and only if the count of all nodes with arcs to themselves is 0.

```
nonreflexive :- evaluate(countofall(X,edge(X,X)),0)
```

With this approach, we do not need to define a helper relation as in the version above. However, it involves the use of an aggregate operator, which some people find more complicated.

9.6 EXERCISES

9.1. Two people are siblings if and only if they share a common parent. Write rules defining the binary `sibling` relation in terms of the `parent` relation. (Hint: you will need the built-in relation `distinct` to get the definition of `sibling` correct.)

9.2. Write rules defining the binary `uncle` relation and the binary `aunt` relation in terms of `parent` and `male` and `female`.

9.3. Two blocks are at the same height if and only if they are resting on the same number of blocks. Define the `sameheight` relation in terms of `block` and `on` in such a way that it works no matter how many blocks there are in the Blocks World.

9.4. Define multiplication `mul` for Modular Arithmetic in terms of `number` and `next`. To simplify the task, you may define additional predicates in terms of `number` and `next`.

9.5. Consider a directed graph defined with a unary relation `node` and a binary base relation `edge`. Write rules to determine if the graph is *asymmetric*, i.e., if there is an arc from one node to a second node, then the graph does not contain an arc from the second to the first.

9.6. Consider a directed graph defined with a unary relation `node` and a binary base relation `edge`. Write rules to to determine if the graph is *symmetric*, i.e., if there is an arc from one node to a second node, then there is also an arc from the second to the first.

9.7. Consider a directed graph defined with a unary relation `node` and a binary base relation `edge`. Write rules to to determine if the graph is *transitive*, i.e., whenever there is an arc from x to y and an arc from y to z, then there is an arc from x to z.

9.8. Consider a directed graph defined with a unary relation `node` and a binary base relation `edge`. Write rules to to determine if the graph is *acyclic*, i.e., there is no sequence of arcs connecting a node to itself.

CHAPTER 10

Lists, Sets, Trees

10.1 INTRODUCTION

In this chapter, we begin our look at view definitions involving constructors and compound terms. The examples here concern the representation of information about lists and trees and sets. In the chapters that follow, we look at the representation of information about dynamic systems and the representation of metaknowledge (i.e., information about information).

10.2 EXAMPLE – PEANO ARITHMETIC

Peano Arithmetic is that branch of Mathematics having to do with the non-negative integers, the function of addition, and the *less than* relation.

Peano Arithmetic is more complicated than Modular Arithmetic in that we have infinitely many objects to consider, viz. the integers 0, 1, 2, 3, ... Since there are infinitely many such numbers, we need infinitely many terms to describe them in our language.

One way to get infinitely many terms is by expanding our vocabulary to include infinitely many symbols. Unfortunately, this would make the job of defining arithmetic impossible, as we would have to write out infinitely many sentences.

Fortunately, there is a better way. In particular, we can represent numbers using a single symbol (e.g., `0`) and a single unary constructor (e.g., `s`). In this approach, we represent the number 0 with the symbol `0`, and we represent every other natural number *n* by applying the constructor `s` exactly *n* times. For example, in this encoding, `s(0)` represents 1; `s(s(0))` represents 2; `s(s(s(0)))` represents 3; and so forth. With this encoding, we automatically get an infinite set of ground terms.

Unfortunately, even with this representation, defining Peano Arithmetic is more challenging than defining Modular Arithmetic. We cannot write all of the facts to characterize addition and multiplication and so forth, because there are infinitely many cases to consider. For Peano Arithmetic, we must rely on view definitions, not just because they are more economical but because they are the only way we can characterize these concepts in finite space.

Let's look at the `number` predicate first. The rules shown here define the `number` relation in terms of `0` and `s`.

```
number(0)
number(s(X)) :- number(X)
```

The next predicate holds of any natural number and the number that follows it. For example, we have next(0,s(0)) and next(s(0),s(s(0))) and so forth. We can define next in general as shown below.

```
next(X,s(X)) :- number(X)
```

Once we have number and next, we can define the usual arithmetic relations. For example, the following sentences define the add relation. Adding 0 to any number results in that number. If adding a number X to a number Y produces a number Z, then adding the successor of X to Y produces the successor of Z.

```
add(0,Y,Y) :- number(Y)
add(s(X),Y,s(Z)) :- add(X,Y,Z)
```

Using next, we can also define the *less than* relation in an analogous manner. A number X is less than a number Z if next holds of X and Z *or* if there is a number Y such that Y is the number after X and Y is less than Z.

```
less(X,Z) :- next(X,Z)
less(X,Z) :- next(X,Y) & less(Y,Z)
```

Before we leave our discussion of arithmetic, it is instructive to look at the concept of Diophantine equations. A *polynomial equation* is a sentence composed using only addition, multiplication, and exponentiation with fixed exponents (that is numbers not variables). For example, the expression shown below in traditional math notation is a polynomial equation.

$$x^2 + 2y = 4z$$

A *natural Diophantine equation* is a polynomial equation in which the variables are restricted to the non-negative integers. For example, the polynomial equation here is also a Diophantine equation and happens to have a solution in the non-negative numbers, viz. $x = 4$ and $y = 8$ and $z = 8$.

Diophantine equations can be readily expressed as sentences in Peano Arithmetic. For example, we can represent the Diophantine equation above with the rule shown below.

```
solution(X,Y,Z) :-
    mul(X,X,X2) &
    mul(s(s(0)),Y,2Y) &
    mul(s(s(s(s(0)))),Z,4Z) &
    add(X2,2Y,4Z)
```

This is a little messy, but it is doable. And we can always clean things up by adding a little syntactic sugar to our notation to make it look like traditional math notation.

10.3 LISTS

A list is a finite sequence of objects. Lists can be flat, e.g., [a, b, f(c), d]. Lists can also be nested within other lists, e.g., [a, [b, f(c)], d].

To talk about lists of arbitrary length, we use the binary constructor cons, and we use the symbol nil to refer to the empty list. In particular, a term of the form cons(τ_1, τ_2) designates a list in which τ_1 denotes the first element and τ_2 denotes the rest of the list.

For example, using this approach, we can represent the list [a, b, c] with the compound term shown below.

cons(a, cons(b, cons(c, nil)))

Rules defining primitives and lists.

```
primitive(a)
primitive(b)
primitive(c)

list(nil)
list(cons(X,Y)) :- object(X) & list(Y)

object(X) :- primitive(X)
object(X) :- list(X)
```

The advantage of this representation is that it allows us to describe relations on lists without regard to length or depth.

As an example, consider the definition of the binary relation mem, which holds of an object and a list if the object is a top-level mem of the list. Using the constructor cons, we can characterize the mem relation as shown below. Obviously, an object is a mem of a list if it is the first element; however, it is also a mem if it is mem of the rest of the list.

```
mem(X,cons(X,Y)) :- object(X) & list(Y)
mem(X,cons(Y,Z)) :- object(Y) & mem(X,Z)
```

In similar fashion, we can define other relations on lists. For example, the following rules define a relation called app. The value of app (its last argument) is a list consisting of the elements in the list supplied as its first argument followed by the elements in the list supplied as its second. For example, we would have app(cons(a,nil), cons(b, cons(c, nil)), cons(a, cons(b, cons(c, nil)))).

```
app(nil,Y,Y) :- list(Y)
app(cons(X,Y),Z,cons(X,W)) :- object(X) & app(Y,Z,W)
```

Finally, a note on syntax. There are three ways to write lists—using square brackets, using `cons`, and using the `!` operator.

If we know all of the elements of a list, we can write the list by wrapping the elements in square brackets and separating them with commas, as in the example shown below.

```
[a,b,c]
```

This list can also be represented using the cons constructor, as shown below.

```
cons(a, cons(b, cons(c, nil)))
```

In order to abbreviate the representation of lists, we can alternatively use the `!` operator in place of cons. For example, we would write the list just discussed as shown below.

```
a!b!c!nil
```

All three of these representations are equivalent. In fact, they typically parse into the same internal representation. However, they each have value in different circumstances, and so all three are permitted.

Lists are an extremely versatile representational device, and the reader is encouraged to become as familiar as possible with the techniques of writing definitions for relations on lists. As is true of many tasks, practice is the best approach to gaining skill.

10.4 EXAMPLE – SORTED LISTS

A *sorted list* is a list in which successive elements satisfy a given ordering relation. For example, the list `[1,2,3]` is a sorted list with "less than" as the ordering relation, while `[1,3,2]` is not.

Note that it is common for objects to appear more than once in a sorted list. For example, `[1,2,2,3]` is a sorted list with "less than or equal" as the ordering relation. However, this cannot happen if the ordering relation is not reflexive. For example, `[1,2,2,3]` is not a sorted list with "less than" as the ordering relation.

Given an ordering relation (e.g., the "less than or equal" relation `leq`), we can easily define a predicate `sorted` that is true of sorted lists and false of everything else. See below. The empty list is sorted. Any list of one element is sorted. A list of two or more elements is sorted if the first element is less than or equal to the second and the tail of the list is sorted.

```
sorted(nil)
sorted([X]) :- object(X)
sorted(cons(X,cons(Y,L))) :- leq(X,Y) & sorted(cons(Y,L))
```

As with unsorted lists, we can define relations on sorted lists as well. However, in doing so we must ensure that the resulting lists are sorted. Although the app relation defined earlier can be applied to sorted lists, the result may not be sorted.

One way to deal with this is to apply a sorter to a list to ensure that it is sorted. For example, the following view definition defines a sorting relation `sortappend` in terms of `app` and `sort`.

```
sortappend(X,Y,Z) :- app(X,Y,W) & sort(W,Z)
```

This approach works, and it yields the correct answer (even when the input lists are not sorted). However, if we know that the input lists are sorted, it is possible to define a sorting relation in another way.

```
merge(nil,Y,Y) :- list(Y)
merge(X!L,Y,Z) :- merge(L,Y,W) & insert(X,W,Z)
```

For many people, this version is more appropriate than the version above. Moreover, as we shall see when we get to program execution, it may execute more efficiently than the preceding version.

10.5 EXAMPLE – SETS

A set is a collection of objects. A set differs from a list in two ways. (1) Objects can appear in lists more than once whereas this cannot happen in a set. (2) The order of elements in a list is essential whereas order is irrelevant for sets.

In what follows, we represent sets as ordered lists. Since order is irrelevant in a set, it does not matter which order we choose, and keeping things ordered makes it easier to define certain relations on sets; and, as we shall see in later lessons, it makes query answering more efficient.

If we represent sets as lists, we can see whether an object is a member of the set using the `mem` relation defined earlier. However, if we represent sets as ordered lists, there is a better way. See below.

```
mem(X,X!L) :- list(L)
mem(X,Y!L) :- less(Y,X) & mem(X,L)
```

As with the definition of list membership, this version loops through the elements of the set. Also, if we get to a subset with the object as the first element, then we terminate successfully. The main difference here is that we can sometimes stop early if an object is not an element of the set. In particular, if, in looping through sublists of the sublist, we get to a sublist in which the specified object is less than the first element, then we can stop searching since we know that all subsequent objects in the list are greater than that element.

One set is a subset of another if and only if every element of the first set is an element of the second. We can define the `subset` relation as shown below.

```
subset(nil,Y) :- list(Y)
subset(X!L,Y) :- mem(X,Y) & subset(L,Y)
```

The intersection two sets is the set consisting of all objects that appear in both sets.

```
intersection(nil,Y,nil) :- list(Y)
intersection(X!L,Y,X!Z) :- mem(X,Y) & intersection(L,Y,Z)
intersection(X!L,Y,Z) :- ~mem(X,Y) & intersection(L,Y,Z)
```

The union of two sets is the set consisting of all elements in either set. If we represent sets as sorted lists, then union is identical to the merge relation defined earlier.

10.6 EXAMPLE – TREES

The cons relation can also be used to represent arbitrary trees. For example, cons(cons(a,b),cons(c,d)) represents a binary tree with a, b, c, and d as leaves.

The among relation is true of an object and a tree if the object is appears somewhere in the tree.

```
among(X,X) :- object(X)
among(X,cons(Y,Z)) :- among(X,Y)
among(X,cons(Y,Z)) :- among(X,Z)
```

Note that, if the specified object is itself a tree, this relation is the same as the subtree relation on trees.

10.7 EXERCISES

10.1. Say whether each of the following sentences is in the extension of the app relation defined in Section 10.3.

(a) app(nil,nil,nil)

(b) app(cons(a,nil),nil,cons(a,nil))

(c) app(cons(a,nil),cons(b,nil),cons(a,b))

(d) app(cons(cons(a,nil),nil),cons(b,nil),cons(a,cons(b,nil)))

10.2. last is a binary relation that holds of an object and a list if and only if the specified object is the *last* element of the specified list. For example, last(c,[a,b,c]) is true. Write a logic program that defines the last relation.

10.3. `rev` is a binary relation on lists. The relation holds of two lists if and only if the second contains the same elements as the first except in the opposite order. For example, `rev([a,b,c],[c,b,a])` is true. Write a logic program that defines the rev relation. Hint: It helps to define a variation on app and then use that variation in defining `rev`.

10.4. `delete` is a ternary relation that holds of an object and two lists if and only if the second list is a copy of the first list with all occurrences of the given object deleted. For example, `delete(b,[a,b,c,b,d],[a,c,d])` is true. Write a logic program that defines the `delete` relation.

10.5. `substitute` is a 4-ary relation that holds of two objects and two lists if and only if the second list is a copy of the first list with all occurrences of the second object replaced by the first object. For example, `substitute(b,d,[a,d,d,c],[a,b,b,c])` is true. Write a logic program that defines the `substitute` relation.

10.6. `adjacent` is a ternary relation that holds of two objects and a list if and only if the first object and the second object are adjacent to each other in the specified list. For example, `adjacent(b,c,[a,b,c,d])` is true. Write a logic program that defines the `adjacent` relation.

10.7. `sublist` is a binary relation that holds of two lists if and only if the first list is a contiguous sublist of the second. For example, `sublist([b,c],[a,b,c,d])` is true while `sublist([b,d],[a,b,c,d])` is not. Write a logic program that defines the `sublist` relation.

10.8. `sort` is a binary relation that holds of two lists if and only if the second list is a version of the first in sorted order. For example, `sort([2,1,3,2],[1,2,2,3])` is true. Write a logic program that defines the `sort` relation in terms of `min`.

10.9. `powerset` is a binary relation that holds of two sets if and only if the second set is the powerset of the first set, i.e., the second is the set of all subsets of the first set. For example, `powerset([a,b],[[],[a],[b],[a,b]])` is true. Write a logic program that defines the `powerset` relation.

CHAPTER 11

Dynamic Systems

11.1 INTRODUCTION

A dynamic system is one that changes state over time. In some cases, the changes occur in response to purely internal events (such as the ticks of a clock). In some cases, these changes are prompted by external inputs. In this chapter, we look at the use of Logic Programming to model purely reactive systems, i.e., those that change in response to external inputs.

Once again consider the Blocks World introduced in Chapter 2. One state of the Blocks World is shown below. Here block C is on block A, block A is on block B, and block E is on block D.

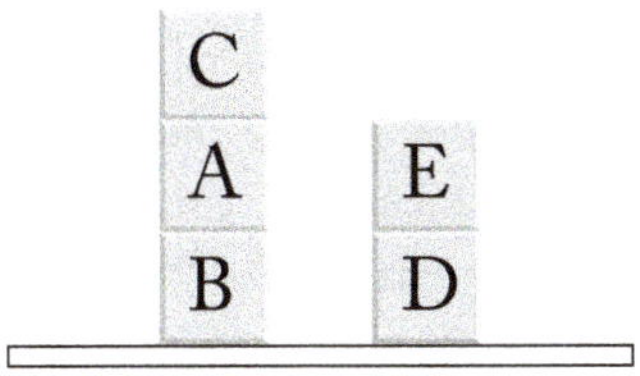

Now, let's consider a dynamic variation of this world, one in which we have operations that can modify the state of the world. For example, unstacking C from A results in the state shown below on the left, and unstacking E from D results in the state shown on the right.

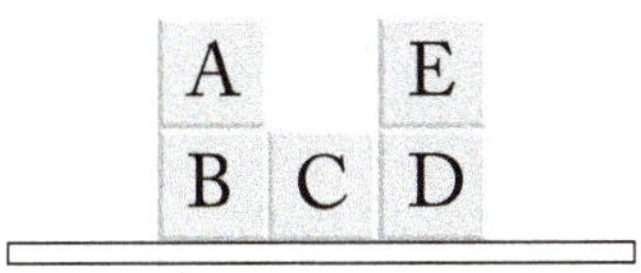

In this chapter, we look at a common way of modeling the behavior of systems like this. In the next section, we introduce fluents (facts that change truth value from one state to another; we then look at actions (inputs that cause such state changes); and, in the section after that, we look at how to write view rules that define the effects of actions on fluents. Given this axiomatization, we then show how to simulate the effects of actions and we show how to plan sequences of actions that lead to desirable states.

11.2 REPRESENTATION

In Chapter 9, we saw how to describe the state of the Blocks World as a dataset using the unary relation `block` and the binary relation on, and we saw how to define others relations, such as `clear` and `table` in terms of these base relations.

Unfortunately, this representation is insufficient for describing dynamic behavior. In a dynamic version of the Blocks World, the properties of blocks and their relationships change over time, and we have to take this into account. Fortunately, we can do this by slightly modifying the items in our previous vocabulary and adding in a few additional items.

First of all, we add a symbol `s1` to our language to stand for the initial state of the world. We could also add symbols for other states of the world; but, as we shall see in the next section, we can refer to these other states in more convenient way.

Second, we introduce a notion of a fluent and provide a suitable representation. A *fluent* is a condition that can change truth value from one state to the next. In our formalization, we take the ground atoms of our static representation to be fluents. However, we now treat them as *terms* instead of factoids. For example, we now treat `on(a,b)` and `clear(a)` as terms rather than as factoids. They are no longer conditions that are always true or false; they are now terms that are true in some states and false in others.

In order to talk about the truth of fluents in specific states, we introduce the binary predicate `tr` and use it to capture the fact that a specified fluent is true in a specified state.

For example, we can represent the initial state of the world shown above with the sentences shown below. Block `c` is on block `a` in state `s1`; block `a` is on block `b`; and so forth.

```
tr(clear(c),s1)
tr(on(c,a),s1)
tr(on(a,b),s1)
tr(table(b),s1)
tr(clear(e),s1)
tr(on(e,d),s1)
tr(table(d),s1)
```

In order to talk about actions that can change the world, we introduce constructors, one for each action. For example, in our Blocks World setting, we would add two new binary constructors u and `s`. `u(X,Y)` represents the action of unstacking block `X` from block `Y`, and `s(X,Y)` represents the action of stacking block `X` onto block `Y`.

In order to define the effects of our actions, we add a binary constructor `do` to talk about the result of performing a given action in a given state. For example, we would write `do(u(c,a),s1)` to refer to the state that results from performing action `u(c,a)` in state `s1`.

To capture the physics of the world, we write rules that say how the world changes as a result of performing each of our actions. See below.

```
tr(table(X),do(u(X,Y),S)) :- tr(clear(X),S) & tr(on(X,Y),S)
tr(clear(Y),do(u(X,Y),S)) :- tr(clear(X),S) & tr(on(X,Y),S)

tr(on(X,Y),do(s(X,Y),S)) :-
  tr(clear(X),S) & tr(table(X),S) & tr(clear(Y),S)
```

Note that, in addition to describing *changes*, we also need to write sentences that records *inertia* (what stays the same). For example, if we unstack one block from another, all blocks that were clear remain clear; all blocks that were on the table remain on the table; and all blocks that were on top of each other remain on top of each other *except* for the blocks involved in the unstacking operation. The following sentences capture the inertial behavior of the Blocks World.

```
tr(clear(U),do(u(X,Y),S)) :- tr(clear(U),S)
tr(table(U),do(u(X,Y),S)) :- tr(table(U),S)
tr(on(U,V),do(u(X,Y),S)) :- tr(on(U,V),S) & distinct(U,X)
tr(on(U,V),do(u(X,Y),S)) :- tr(on(U,V),S) & distinct(V,Y)

tr(clear(U),do(s(X,Y),S)) :- tr(clear(U),S) & distinct(U,Y)
tr(table(U),do(s(X,Y),S)) :- tr(table(U),S) & distinct(U,X)
tr(on(U,V),do(s(X,Y),S)) :- tr(on(U,V),S)
```

Sentences like these, which express what *remains the same*, are often called *frame axioms*. Many people are irked by the need to formalize what remains the same in representing dynamics. Luckily, there are alternative ways of formalizing dynamics that eliminates the need for frame axioms. For example, instead of formalizing what is *true* in the state that results from performing an action, we can formalize what *changes* from the current state (in the form of *add* lists and *delete* lists). See Chapter 14 for more discussion of this technique.

11.3 SIMULATION

Simulation is the process of determining the state that results from the execution of a given action of sequence of actions in a given state. Once we have a representation of the physics of our world, simulation is easy.

As an example, consider the initial state described in the preceding section, and consider the following sequence of two actions. We first unstack c from a, and we then stack c onto e. If we were interested in the state of affairs after the execution of these actions, we could write the query shown below.

```
goal(P) :- tr(P,do(s(c,d),do(u(c,a),s1)))
```

The initial state is shown below, once again.

```
tr(clear(c),s1)
tr(on(c,a),s1)
tr(on(a,b),s1)
tr(table(b),s1)
tr(clear(e),s1)
tr(on(e,d),s1)
tr(table(d),s1)
```

Using this data and the change rules and frame axioms, we see that executing `u(c,a)` in this state results in the data shown below.

```
tr(clear(c),do(u(c,a),s1))
tr(table(c),do(u(c,a),s1))
tr(clear(a),do(u(c,a),s1))
tr(on(a,b),do(u(c,a),s1))
tr(table(b),do(u(c,a),s1))
tr(clear(e),do(u(c,a),s1))
tr(on(e,d),do(u(c,a),s1))
tr(table(d),do(u(c,a),s1))
```

Applying the change rules and frame rules once again, we get the following conclusions.

```
tr(clear(c),do(s(c,e),do(u(c,a),s1)))
tr(on(c,e),do(s(c,e),do(u(c,a),s1)))
tr(clear(a),do(s(c,e),do(u(c,a),s1)))
tr(on(a,b),do(s(c,e),do(u(c,a),s1)))
tr(table(b),do(s(c,e),do(u(c,a),s1)))
tr(on(e,d),do(s(c,e),do(u(c,a),s1)))
tr(table(d),do(s(c,e),do(u(c,a),s1)))
```

Finally, using the rule defining the `goal` predicate, we end up with the data shown below.

```
goal(clear(c))
goal(on(c,e))
goal(clear(a))
goal(on(a,b))
goal(table(b))
```

```
goal(on(e,d))
goal(table(d))
```

The partial results shown above make his process look complicated, but in reality the process is fairly simple and not very expensive. Finding a plan to achieve a goal state is not so simple.

11.4 PLANNING

Planning is in some ways the opposite of simulation. In simulation, we start with an *initial state* and a *plan*, i.e., a sequence of actions; and we use simulation to determine the result of executing the plan in the initial state. In planning, we start with an initial state and a *goal*, i.e., a set of desirable states; and we use planning to compute a plan that achieves one of the goal states.

In what follows, we again use the unary predicate `goal`, except, in this case, we define it to be true of desired states rather than fluents as in the formalization in the last section. For example, the following rule defines `goal` to be true of a state if and only if the fluents `on(a,b)` and `on(b,c)` are true in that state.

```
goal(S) :- tr(on(a,b),S) & tr(on(b,c),S)
```

Using this definition of `goal` and the rules in Section 11.4, it is easy to see that the following conclusion is true, i.e., `on(a,b)` and `on(b,c)` are both true in state `do(s(a,b),do(s(b,c),do(u(a,b),do(u(c,a),s1))))`, i.e., the state that results from unstacking `c`, unstacking `a`, stacking `b` onto `c`, and stacking `a` onto `b`.

```
goal(do(s(a,b),do(s(b,c),do(u(a,b),do(u(c,a),s1)))))
```

In principle, we should be able to derive this conclusion through bottom-up or top-down evaluation. Unfortunately, bottom-up evaluation explores many plans that have nothing to do with the goals. Top-down evaluation stays focussed on the goal. Unfortunately, with the rules shown above, it is likely to go into an infinite loop, exploring longer and longer plans when the simple four-step plan shown above works.

The solution to this dilemma is to use a hybrid of the two approaches. We define the binary predicate `plan` as shown below. `plan` is true of the empty plan and a state if and only if that state satisfies the goal. It is true of a non-empty sequence of actions if and only if the "tail" of the sequence achieves the goal when executed in the result of applying the first action in the given state.

```
plan(nil,S) :- goal(S)
plan(A!L,S) :- plan(L,do(A,S))
```

Given this definition, we can pose the question `plan(L,s1)`, and top-down evaluation will try plans of increasing length, trying short plans to see if the achieve the goal and moving to longer plans only if none fails to achieve the goal.

This approach is somewhat faster than bottom-up execution and guarantees to produce the shortest possible plan. That said, the method is still expensive. A significant amount of research has been done to find ways to produce plans more effectively. However, it is possible to show that a complete search of the plan space is sometimes needed.

11.5 EXERCISES

11.1. Suppose we wanted to augment the Blocks World with an action `move(X,Y,Z)` that moves block `X` from block `Y` to block `Z`. Write the change axioms and frame axioms for this new action in terms of the vocabulary introduced in this chapter.

11.2. Given the change and frame axioms in this chapter and the data shown below, evaluate the query `goal(P) :- tr(P,do(s(b,e),do(u(a,b),do(u(c,a),s1))))`.

```
tr(clear(c),s1)
tr(on(c,a),s1)
tr(on(a,b),s1)
tr(table(b),s1)
tr(clear(e),s1)
tr(on(e,d),s1)
tr(table(d),s1)
```

11.3. Assuming the change axioms and frame axioms and goal definition in this chapter and the data shown below, give one answer to the query `result([X,Y]) :- plan([X,Y],s2)`.

```
tr(clear(a),s2)
tr(table(a),s2)
tr(clear(b),s2)
tr(on(b,c),s2)
tr(table(c),s2)
tr(clear(e),s2)
tr(on(e,d),s2)
tr(table(d),s2)
```

CHAPTER 12

Metaknowledge

12.1 INTRODUCTION

One of the interesting features of our language is that it allows us to encode information about information. The trick is to represent *sentences* as *terms* in our language and then write sentences about these terms, thereby effectively writing sentences about sentences. There are numerous uses of this technique. In this chapter, we look at two of these—describing the syntax and semantics of other languages within our language and representing Boolean Logic within Logic Programming.

12.2 NATURAL LANGUAGE PROCESSING

Pseudo English is a formal language that is intended to approximate the syntax of the English language. One way to define the syntax of Pseudo English is to write grammatical rules in Backus Naur Form (BNF). The rules shown below illustrate this approach for a small subset of Pseudo English. A sentence is a noun phrase followed by a verb phrase. A noun phrase is either a noun or two nouns separated by the word `and`. A verb phrase is a verb followed by a noun phrase. A noun is either the word `mary` or the word `pat` or the word `quincy`. A verb is either `like` or `likes`.

```
<sentence> ::= <np> <vp>
<np> ::= <noun>
<np> ::= <noun> "and" <noun>
<vp> ::= <verb> <np>
<noun> ::= "mary" | "pat" | "quincy"
<verb> ::= "like" | "likes"
```

Alternatively, we can use rules to formalize the syntax of Pseudo English. The sentences shown below express the grammar described in the BNF rules above. Here, we are using the app relation to talk about the result of appending words.

```
sentence(Z) :- np(X) & vp(Y) & app(X,Y,Z)
np(X) :- noun(X)
np(W) :- noun(X) & noun(Y) & app(X,and,Z) & app(Z,Y,W)
```

```
vp(Z) :- verb(X) & np(Y) & app(X,Y,Z)
noun(mary)
noun(pat)
noun(quincy)
verb(like)
verb(likes)
```

Using these rules, we can test whether a given sequence of words is a syntactically legal sentence in Pseudo English and we can enumerate syntactically legal sentences, like those shown below.

```
mary likes pat
pat and quincy like mary
mary likes pat and quincy
```

One weakness of our BNF and the corresponding axiomatization is that there is no concern for agreement in number between subjects and verbs. Hence, with these rules, we can get the following expressions, which are ungrammatical in Natural English.

```
x   mary like pat
x   pat and quincy likes mary
```

Fortunately, we can fix this problem by elaborating our rules just a bit. In particular, we can add an argument to some of our relations to indicate whether the expression is singular or plural, and we can then use this to block sequences of words where the numbers do not agree.

```
sentence(Z) :- np(X,W) & vp(Y,W) & app(X,Y,Z)

np(X,singular) :- noun(X)
np(W,plural) :- noun(X) & noun(Y) & app(X,and,Z) & app(Z,Y,W)

vp(Z,W) :- verb(X,W) & np(Y,V) & app(X,Y,Z)

noun(mary)
noun(pat)
noun(quincy)

verb(like,plural)
verb(likes,singular)
```

With these rules, the syntactically correct sentences shown above are still guaranteed to be sentences, but the ungrammatical sequences are blocked. Other grammatical features can be formalized in similar fashion, e.g., gender agreement in pronouns (`he` versus `she`), possessive adjectives (`his` versus `her`), reflexives (`himself` versus `herself`), and so forth.

12.3 BOOLEAN LOGIC

Throughout this volume, we have been using English to talk about Logic Programming. A natural question to ask is whether it is possible formalize Logic Programming within Logic Programming. The answer is yes, but there are some limits to what can be done.

In this section, we look at a simple version of this problem, viz. using Logic Programming to formalize the syntax and semantics of Boolean Logic. Sentences in Boolean Logic are simpler than those in Logic Programming. The vocabulary consists of atomic *propositions*, and sentences are either propositions or complex expressions formed from *logical operators*. The sentence shown below is an example. This is a statement that either p is true and q is false or p is false and q is true.

$$(p \wedge \neg q) \vee (\neg p \wedge q)$$

In what follows, we associate a symbol with each proposition in our Boolean Logic language. For example, we use `p`, `q`, and `r` to represent proposition p, q, and r.

Next, we introduce constructors o form complex sentences. There is one constructor for each logical operator—`not` for $\neg$, `and` for $\wedge$, and `or` for $\vee$. Using these constructors, we can represent Boolean Logic sentences as terms in our language. For example, we could represent the sentence above as follows.

```
or(and(p,not(q)),and(not(p),q))
```

Finally, we introduce a selection of predicates to express the types of various expressions in our Boolean Logic language. We use the unary predicate `proposition` to assert that an expression is a proposition. We use the unary predicate `negation` to assert that an expression is a negation. We use the unary predicate `conjunction` to assert that an expression is a conjunction. We use the unary predicate `disjunction` to assert that an expression is a disjunction. And we use the unary predicate `sentence` to assert that an expression is a sentence.

With this vocabulary, we can characterize the syntax of our language as follows. We start with declarations of our proposition constants.

```
proposition(p)
proposition(q)
proposition(r)
```

Next, we define the types of expressions involving logical operators.

```
negation(not(X)) :- sentence(X)
conjunction(and(X,Y)) :- sentence(X) & sentence(Y)
disjunction(or(X,Y)) :- sentence(X) & sentence(Y)
```

Finally, we define sentences as expressions of these types.

```
sentence(X) :- proposition(X)
sentence(X) :- negation(X)
sentence(X) :- conjunction(X)
sentence(X) :- disjunction(X)
```

A truth assignment is a mapping from proposition constants to Boolean values (true or false). We can encode a truth assignment with a binary relation `value` that relates a proposition constant and the associated value. For example the following facts constitute a truth assignment for the proposition constants above. In this case, `p` is true, `q` is false, and `r` is true.

```
value(p,true)
value(q,false)
value(r,true)
```

Given a truth assignment, we can define a `truth` value for every sentence in our language. A proposition is true if and only if it is assigned the value `true`. A negation is true if and only if its argument is false. A conjunction is true if and only if both conjuncts are true. A disjunction is true if and only if at least one of its disjuncts is true.

```
truth(P) :- value(P,true)
truth(not(P)) :- ~truth(P)
truth(and(P,Q)) :- truth(P) & truth(Q)
truth(or(P,Q)) :- truth(P)
truth(or(P,Q)) :- truth(Q)
```

We can make our formalization more interesting by reifying truth assignments as objects. We could then talk about properties of sentences such as validity and satisfiability. A sentence is valid if and only if it is true in every truth assignment. A sentence is satisfiable if and only if some truth assignment satisfies it. A sentence is falsifiable if and only if some truth assignment makes it false. A sentence is unsatisfiable if and only if no truth assignment makes it true.

12.4 EXERCISES

12.1. Suppose we were to add the words `himself` and `herself` to the grammar in section of Pseudo English. Modify the rules defining our Pseudo English grammar so that these words appear only as the objects of sentences and so that, when one of these words is used in a sentence, its number and gender corresponds to the number and gender of the subject of that sentence.

12.2. Say whether each of the following sentences is a consequence of the sentences in the section on Boolean Logic.

(a) `conjunction(and(not(p),not(q)))`

(b) `conjunction(not(or(not(p),not(q))))`

(c) `sentence(not(not(p)))`

(d) `sentence(or(not(p),not(q),not(r)))`

(d) `sentence(and(p,not(p))`

12.3. Which of the following sentences are consequences of the truth assignment and rules in the section on Boolean Logic?

(a) `truth(or(not(p),not(q)))`

(b) `truth(not(and(not(p),not(q))))`

(c) `truth(and(p,not(p))`

12.4. Suppose we wanted to add the `xor` operator to our Boolean Logic language. `xor(p,q)` is true if and only if the valuation of `p` is *different* from the valuation of `q`. Write a rule to extend our definition of `truth` to accommodate the `xor` operator.

PART IV

Operation Definitions

CHAPTER 13

Operations

13.1 INTRODUCTION

In the preceding unit (Chapters 7–12), we saw how to write rules to define *view relations* in terms of base relations. Once defined, we can use those views in queries and in the definitions of other views.

In this unit (Chapters 13–16), we look at how to write rules that define *operations* in terms of changes to base relations. Once defined, we can use those operations in updates and in the definitions of other operations.

As we have seen, the rules used in writing view definitions generalize the rules used in writing queries; and, as we shall see, the rules used in writing operation definitions generalize the rules used in writing updates. That said, it is important to keep in mind the differences between views and operations—views are used in talking about *facts* that are true in states whereas operations are used in talking about *changes* to states.

In this chapter, we define the syntax and semantics of operation definitions. In the next chapter, we see how operation definitions can be used to specify the handling of events in dynamic systems (where the system's behavior changes in response to external stimuli). In Chapter 15, we look at how to use operation definitions in database management. And, in Chapter 16, we look at how to use operation definitions in building interactive worksheets.

13.2 SYNTAX

The syntax of operation definitions builds upon the syntax of updates described in Chapter 4. The various types of constants are the same, and the notions of term and atom and literal are also the same. However, to these, we add a few new items.

To denote operations, we designate some constants as *operation constants*. As with constructors and relation constants, each operation constant has a fixed arity—unary, binary, and so forth.

An *action* is an application of an operation to specific objects. In what follows, we denote actions using a syntax similar to that of atomic sentences, viz. an n-ary operation constant followed by n terms enclosed in parentheses and separated by commas. For example, if `f` is a binary operation constant and `a` and `b` are symbols, then `f(a,b)` denotes the action of applying the operation `f` to `a` and `b`.

An *operation definition rule* (or, more simply, an *operation rule*) is an expression of the form shown below. Each rule consists of (1) an action expression, (2) a double colon, (3) a literal or a conjunction of literals, (4) a double-shafted forward arrow, and (5) a literal or an action expression or a conjunction of literals and action expressions. The action expression to the left of the double colon is called the *head*; the literals to the left of the arrow are called *conditions*; and the literals to its right are called *effects*.

$$\gamma \;\; :: \;\; [\sim]\phi_1 \;\&\ldots\&\; [\sim]\phi_m \;\; ==> \;\; [\sim]\psi_1 \;\&\ldots\&\; [\sim]\psi_n \;\&\; \gamma_1 \;\&\ldots\&\; \gamma_k$$

Intuitively, the meaning of an operation rule is simple. If the conditions of a rule are true in any state, then executing the action in the head requires that we execute the effects of the rule.

For example, the following rule states that in any state in which `p(a,b)` is true and `q(a)` is false, then executing `click(a)` requires that we remove `p(a,b)` from our dataset, add `q(a)`, and perform action `click(b)`.

```
click(a) :: p(a,b) & ~q(a)  ==>  ~p(a,b) & q(a) & click(b)
```

As with rules defining views, operation rules may contain variables to express information in a compact form. For example, we can write the following rule to generalize the preceding rule to all objects.

```
click(X) :: p(X,Y) & ~q(X)  ==>  ~p(X,Y) & q(X) & click(Y)
```

As with view rules, *safety* is a consideration. Safety in this case means that every variable among the effects of a rule or in negative conditions also appears in the head of the rule or in the positive conditions.

The operation rules shown above are both safe. However, the rules shown below are not. The second effect of the first rule contains a variable that does not appear in the head or in any positive condition. In the second rule, there is a variable that appears in a negative condition that does not appear in the head or in any positive condition.

```
click(X) :: p(X,Y) & ~q(X)  ==>  ~p(X,Y) & q(Z) & click(Y)
click(X) :: p(X,Y) & ~q(Z)  ==>  ~p(X,Y) & q(X) & click(Y)
```

In some operation rules there is no condition, i.e., the effects of the transition rule take place on all datasets. We can, of course, write such rules by using the condition `true`, as in the following example.

```
click(X) :: true  ==>  ~p(X) & q(X)
```

For the sake of simplicity in writing our examples, we sometimes abbreviate such rules by dropping the conditions and the transition operator and instead write just the effects of the transition as the body of the operation rule. For example, we can abbreviate the rule above as shown below.

```
click(X) :: ~p(X) & q(X)
```

An *operation definition* is a collection of operation rules in which the same operation appears in the head of every rule. As with view definitions, we are interested primarily in rulesets that are finite. However, in analyzing operation definitions, we occasionally talk about the set of all ground instances of the rules, and in some cases these sets are infinite.

13.3 SEMANTICS

The semantics of operation definitions is more complicated than the semantics of updates due to the possible occurrence of views in the conditions of the rule and the possible occurrence of operations in its effects. In what follows, we first define the expansion of an action in the context of a given dataset, and we then define the result of performing that action on that dataset.

Suppose we are given a set Ω of rules, a set Γ of actions (factoids, negated factoids, and actions), and a dataset Δ. We say that an *instance* of a rule in Ω is *active* with respect to Γ and Δ if and only if the head of the rule is in Γ and the conditions of the rule are all true in Δ.

Given this notion, we define the *expansion* of action γ with respect to rule set Ω and dataset Δ as follows. Let Γ_0 be $\{\gamma\}$ and let Γ_{i+1} be the set of all effects in any instance of any rule in Ω with respect to Γ_i and Δ. We define our expansion $U(\gamma,\Omega,\Delta)$ as the fixpoint of this series. Equivalently, it is the union of the sets Γ_i, for all non-negative integers i.

Next, we define the positive updates $A(\gamma,\Omega,\Delta)$ to be the positive base factoids in $U(\gamma,\Omega,\Delta)$. We define the negative updates $D(\gamma,\Omega,\Delta)$ to be the set of all negative factoids in $U(\gamma,\Omega,\Delta)$.

Finally, we define the result of applying an action γ to a dataset Δ as the result of removing the negative updates from Δ and adding the positive updates, i.e., the result is $(\Delta - D(\gamma,\Omega,\Delta)) \cap A(\gamma,\Omega,\Delta)$.

To illustrate these definitions, consider an application with a dataset representing a directed acyclic graph. In the sentences below, we use symbols to designate the nodes of the graph, and we use the edge relation to designate the arcs of the graph.

```
edge(a,b)
edge(b,d)
edge(b,e)
```

The following operation definition defines a ternary operation copy that copies the outgoing arcs in the graph from its first argument to its second argument.

```
copy(X,Y) :: edge(X,Z)  ==>  edge(Y,Z)
```

Given this operation definition and the dataset shown above, the expansion of copy(b,c) consists of the changes shown below. In this case, the factoids representing the two arcs emanating from b are all copied to c.

```
edge(c,d)
edge(c,e)
```

After executing this event, we end up with the following dataset.

```
edge(a,b)
edge(b,d)
edge(b,e)
edge(c,d)
edge(c,e)
```

The following rule defines a unary operation invert that reverses the incoming arcs of the node specified as it argument.

```
invert(Y) :: edge(X,Y)  ==>  ~edge(X,Y) & edge(Y,X)
```

The expansion of invert(c) is shown below. In this case, the arguments in the factoid with c as second argument have all been reversed.

```
~edge(c,d)
~edge(c,e)
edge(d,c)
edge(e,c)
```

After executing this event, we end up with the following dataset.

```
edge(a,b)
edge(b,d)
edge(b,e)
edge(d,c)
edge(e,c)
```

Finally, the following operation rules define a binary operation that inserts a new node into the graph (the first argument) with an arc to the second argument and arcs to all of the nodes that are reachable from the second argument.

```
insert(X,Y) :: edge(X,Y)
insert(X,Y) :: edge(Y,Z) ==> insert(X,Z)
```

The expansion of `insert(w,b)` is shown below. The first rule adds `edge(w,b)` to the expansion. The second rule adds `insert(w,d)` and `insert(w,e)`. Given these events, on the next round of expansion, the first rule adds `edge(w,d)` and `edge(w,e)` and the second rules adds `insert(w,c)`. On the third round of expansion, we get `edge(w,c)`. At this point, neither rule adds any additional items to our expansion, and the process terminates.

```
insert(w,b)
edge(w,b)
insert(w,d)
insert(w,e)
edge(w,d)
edge(w,e)
insert(w,c)
edge(w,c)
```

Applying this event to the preceding dataset produces the result shown below.

```
edge(a,b)
edge(b,d)
edge(b,e)
edge(d,c)
edge(e,c)
edge(w,b)
edge(w,d)
edge(w,e)
edge(w,c)
```

Note that it is possible to define `insert` in other ways. We could, for example, define a view of `edge` that relates each node to every node that can be reached from the node; and we could then use this view in a non-recursive definition of `insert`. However, this would require us to introduce a new view into our vocabulary; and, for many people, this is less clear than the definition shown above.

13.4 EXERCISES

13.1. For each of the following strings, say whether it is a syntactically legal operation definition.

(a) `a(X) :: p(X,Y) ==> q(Y,X)`

(b) `a(X) :: p(X,Y) & a(Y) ==> q(Y,X)`

(c) `a(X) :: p(X,Y) ==> q(Y,X) & a(Y)`

(d) `a(X) :: p(X,Y) ==> q(Y,X) & ~a(Y)`

(e) `a(X) :: p(Y,Y) ==> q(X,Y)`

13.2. Say whether each of the following queries is safe.

(a) `a(X) :: p(X,Y) & p(Y,Z) ==> p(X,Z)`

(b) `a(X) :: p(X,Y) & ~p(Y,Z) ==> p(X,Z)`

(c) `a(X) :: p(Y,Z) ==> p(X,Z)`

(d) `a(X) :: p(Y,Z) ==> ~p(X,Z)`

(e) `a(X) :: p(Y,Z) ==> p(Z,Y)`

13.3. Given the definition `fix(X) :- p(X,Y) & p(Y,Z) ==> p(X,Z)`, what is the result of executing the action `fix(a)` on the dataset shown below.

```
p(a,b)
p(b,c)
p(c,d)
p(d,e)
```

13.4. Given the definition `fix(X) :- p(X,Y) & p(Y,Z) ==> p(X,Z) & fix(Y)`, what is the result of executing the action `fix(a)` on the dataset shown below.

```
p(a,b)
p(b,c)
p(c,d)
p(d,e)
```

13.5. Consider a type hierarchy like the one shown below.

```
subtype(giraffe,mammal)
subtype(rabbit,mammal)
subtype(mammal,vertebrate)
subtype(earthworm,vertebrate)
```

```
subtype(vertebrate,animal)
subtype(invertebrate,animal)
```

Define an operation `classify` that takes an object and a type as arguments and adds factoids stating that the object has that type and all supertypes of that type. For example, executing the action `classify(george,giraffe)` should result in the following factoids being added to the dataset.

```
type(george,giraffe)
type(george,mammal)
type(george,vertebrate)
type(george,animal)
```

CHAPTER 14

Dynamic Logic Programs

14.1 INTRODUCTION

In Chapter 11, we saw how to use view definitions to describe the behavior of dynamic systems. In this chapter, we look at an alternative approach using operation definitions. When systems are defined in this way, they are called *dynamic logic programs*.

In the next section, we look at an example of a reactive system, i.e., one that responds to external inputs. We then look at an example of a closed dynamic system, i.e., one that operates without external input. After that, we look at an example of mixed initiative system, i.e., one that is driven by a combination of internal and external stimuli. Finally, we look at the issues involved in handling simultaneous inputs.

14.2 REACTIVE SYSTEMS

The simplest form of reactive system is one whose behavior is driven entirely by external inputs. Prior to an input, the system is quiescent, i.e., nothing is changing; on observing an input, the system changes state in accordance with the input; and, afterward, the system becomes quiescent once again (until the next input is observed).

As an example, consider a system with three buttons and three lights. At each point in time, some of the lights are on and some are off. If the user pushes the first button, the system toggles the first light. If the user pushes the second button, the system interchanges the states of the first light and the second light. If the user pushes the third button, the system interchanges the states of the second and third lights.

In order to formalize the behavior of this system, we give names to the components of state. We use the Boolean predicate `p` to mean that the first light is on; `q` means that the second light is on; and `r` means that the third light is on. Next, we give names to the three possible events. We use the Boolean predicate `a` to designate the first button being pushed; `b` refers to the second button being pushed; and `c` refers to the third button being pushed.

Given this vocabulary, we represent the state of our system as a dataset consisting of some subset of `p`, `q`, and `r` factoids, and we represent the occurrence of an event as one of our three actions, i.e., `a`, `b`, or `c`.

With this new terminology, we can describe the desired behavior of our system with the operation definitions shown below. If the user pushes the `a` button and `p` is true, the system makes `p` false. If the user pushes `a` and `p` is false, the system makes `p` true. If the user pushes `b`, the system interchanges `p` and `q`. And, if the user pushes `c`, the system interchanges `q` and

r. (Note that, if action b is performed and p and q are the same, nothing changes. Similarly, if action c is performed and q and r are the same, nothing changes. Consequently, we do not need rules for those cases.)

```
a :: p ==> ~p
a :: ~p ==> p
b :: p & ~q ==> ~p & q
b :: ~p & q ==> p & ~q
c :: q & ~r ==> ~q & r
c :: ~q & r ==> q & ~r
```

Note that, if the system starts in a state in which all three conditions are false, it can achieve a state in which they are true by executing the action sequence a, b, c, a, b, and a. Can you think of a different sequence of actions that would do the trick? How many sequences are there that produce the desired state?

14.3 CLOSED SYSTEMS

A closed dynamic system is one that operates without external input. Its behavior results from internal stimuli only, such as the ticks of a clock.

As an example, imagine a variation of the Buttons and Lights World described in the preceding section. In this case, there are no buttons and so no external input. Instead, the system cycles through states, starting in a state where all of the lights are off, cycling through states in a particular order until all lights are on, resetting, and then repeating ad infinitum.

In specifying the behavior of this system, we use the same vocabulary as in the preceding section except that in place of the actions a, b, and c, we have a single internal action tick representing the tick of the clock.

With this terminology, we can describe the desired behavior of our system with the operation definition shown below. When the clock ticks, the system changes state in accordance with the state current at that time. When all of the lights are off, the first light is turned on. When the first light is on and only the first light is on, the first light is extinguished and the second light is turned on. And so forth.

```
tick :: ~p & ~q & ~r ==> p & ~q & ~r
tick :: p & ~q & ~r ==> ~p & q & ~r
tick :: ~p & q & ~r ==>  ~p & ~q & r
tick :: ~p & ~q & r ==>  p & ~q & r
tick :: p & ~q & r ==> ~p & q & r
tick :: ~p & q & r ==> p & q & r
tick :: p & q & r ==> ~p & ~q & ~r
```

Note that this sequence of states is the same as the sequence that would result by executing the sequence of actions mentioned at the end of the preceding section, viz. a, b, c, a, b, and a.

If we wanted, we could also formalize this behavior using the actions defined in the preceding sections (except that the actions would be internal actions, not external stimuli).

As before, we would have the definitions of the actions, but to these we would add a `reset` operation to turn off all of the lights. See below.

```
a :: p ==> ~p
a :: ~p ==> p
b :: p & ~q ==> ~p & q
b :: ~p & q ==> p & ~q
c :: q & ~r ==> ~q & r
c :: ~q & r ==> q & ~r
reset :: ~p & ~q & ~r
```

Given these definitions, we could rewrite the specification above as shown below. The rules have the same conditions; but, instead of enumerating changes to base relations, the rules in this case specify which internal action is performed in which state.

```
tick :: ~p & ~q & ~r ==> a
tick :: p & ~q & ~r ==> b
tick :: ~p & q & ~r ==> c
tick :: ~p & ~q & r ==> a
tick :: p & ~q & r ==> b
tick :: ~p & q & r ==> a
tick :: p & q & r ==> reset
```

This style of specification is sometimes called a *universal plan*. For each state, it specifies an action to be performed in that state.

14.4 MIXED INITIATIVE

A mixed initiative system is one whose behavior is determined by either external or internal inputs. Interestingly, in a mixed initiative system, a single external input can lead to a single state change or a sequence of changes.

As an example, consider a variation of the closed Buttons and Lights World described in the preceding section. In this version, in place of the buttons described in Section 14.2, we have two different buttons. If the user pushes the first button, the system begins behaving as described in the preceding section. If the user presses the second button, the system pauses its operation. If the user presses the first button again, the system picks up where it left off.

As before, we use p, q, and r to describe the state of the three lights. To these, we add a single 0-ary predicate running to capture the state of the process. We use the symbols play and stop, to refer to the two external inputs. Finally, as before, we use the symbol tick to refer to a tick of the internal clock.

The operation rules below specify the desired behavior of our system. The definitions of play and stop, ad there are the usual rules defining tick, the only difference being the dependence on running.

```
play :: running
stop :: ~running

tick :: running & ~p & ~q & ~r ==> p
tick :: running & p & ~q & ~r ==> ~p & q
tick :: running & ~p & q & ~r ==> c
tick :: running & ~p & ~q & r ==> a
tick :: running & p & ~q & r ==> b
tick :: running & ~p & q & r ==> a
tick :: running & p & q & r ==> reset
tick :: running & p & q & r ==> reset
```

Given these rules, the system will exhibit the desired behavior. When the user presses the play button, the state is updated to include the factoid running. The upshot is that, as the system's internal clock ticks, it proceeds through its cycle of states. When the user presses stop button, running is removed, and the system will do nothing on subsequent clock ticks unless the play button is pushed once again.

14.5 SIMULTANEOUS ACTIONS

In the preceding sections, we looked at the problem of handling one input at a time. In some applications, we must deal with the possibility of multiple simultaneous inputs. For example, a robot might be commanded to move and extend its arm at the same time, or a computer user might press two keys at the same time.

In some cases, the effects of such events are independent of each other. In such cases, it is possible to handle such events independently, in effect treating the events as though they happened independently.

The a operation and the c operation in the original version of the Buttons and Lights World illustrate this. The behaviors associated with these inputs are independent of each other. Pressing the a button toggles p and has nothing to do with q and r. Pressing the c button interchanges q and r and has nothing to do with p. The upshot is that these inputs can be processed independently and simultaneously in accordance with the rules defining their individual behaviors.

Unfortunately, treating simultaneous inputs independently does not always work. In some cases, simultaneous actions can interact in ways that lead to results that are different from the results of independent execution.

As an example, consider a state in which the first and second lights in the Buttons and Lights World are both on, and imagine that the user simultaneously presses both the first and second buttons, i.e., he performs actions `a` and `b` at the same time. In this situation, the definition of the `a` action mandates that `p` should become false, and the definition of the `b` action mandates that `p` should become true. So what happens?

The problem in this case is that our operation definitions, as written, assume that only one action occurs at a time. In order to deal with the possible interactions, we need to describe the effects of simultaneous inputs.

One way to do this is to invent terminology for talking about *compound actions* and then write operation definitions for such combinations.

If the number of possible actions is small, it is common practice to use *chords* to specify different combinations of inputs. For example, in the Buttons and Lights World, we could use a ternary constructor `press` and specify Booleans as arguments. If the first argument is `true`, this means that button `a` is pressed. If the second argument is `true`, this means that button `b` is pressed. If the third argument is `true`, this means that button `c` is pressed. By specifying different combinations of Boolean, we can characterize various combinations of actions.

If the number of possible actions is large, representing compound actions as chords is impractical. In such cases, it is common practice to represent compound actions as *action lists*. For example, in the Buttons and Lights World, we would invent represent the combination of actions `a` and `c` with the list `[a,c]`, and we might specify the execution of this compound action by writing an expression like `execute([a,c])`.

Once we have a representation for compound actions, we can write operation definitions using this representation. For example, the rules shown below specify one possible behavior for a Buttons and Lights World system that allows up to two simultaneous actions. If the user presses both `a` and `b` at the same time, then `a` has its usual effect on `p` and `b` has its usual effect on `q`. If the user presses both `a` and `b` at the same time, then these actions have their usual effects (as defined in Section 14.2). If the user presses both `b` and `c` at the same time, then `b` has its usual effect on `q` and `c` has its usual effect on `r`.

```
execute([a,b]) :: ~p ==> p & ~q
execute([a,b]) :: p ==> ~p & q
execute([a,c]) :: a
execute([a,c]) :: c
execute([b,c]) :: q & ~r ==> ~q & r
execute([b,c]) :: ~q & r ==> q & ~r
```

Note that, if all actions in an application are independent of each other, specifying the behavior of compound actions is very simple. Suppose, for example, we had a system with a selection of individual actions `execute(a)`, `execute(b)`, and so forth; and suppose that these actions were all independent. Then we could define the behavior of a system in response to an arbitrary subset of these actions with the rule shown below (together with the rules defining the individual actions).

```
execute(L) :: member(A,L) ==> execute(A)
```

Formalizing the behavior of simultaneous inputs can be tedious. However, using operation definitions for compound actions, it is at least possible to formalize this behavior correctly in situations where independent treatment would be inadequate.

14.6 EXERCISES

14.1. Consider the Buttons and Lights World described in the chapter but in this version assume there is a fourth button `d` that toggles all of the lights at once. Write an operation definition for `d`.

14.2. Rewrite the operation definitions for the Buttons and Lights World to deal with the possibility of simultaneous execution of all three actions `a` and `b` and `c`. Assume that these actions have their usual effects when done independently but result in all three lights turning off when all three buttons are pushed at the same time.

CHAPTER 15

Database Management

15.1 INTRODUCTION

In the preceding chapter, we looked at the process of updating datasets in response to inputs. In this chapter, we look at a special case of this more general process, one where the inputs are additions and deletions of specific facts.

In order to specify such inputs, we use two new operations, viz. `add` and `delete`. `add` takes a ground atom as argument and signifies a request that the specified atom be added to the current dataset. `delete` takes a ground atom as argument and signifies a request that the specified atom be deleted from the current dataset.

Note that a system may or may not act upon the requests it receives. It may also add or delete facts not specified in the input. Operation rules allow the programmer to specify exactly how the database should change in response to inputs.

In this chapter, we look first at the use of operation definitions to ensure that dataset constraints remain satisfied after updates. In the subsequent section, we look at the use of operation definitions to update materialized views. And then we look at the use of operation definitions to specify updates to base relations when given requests for updates to view relations.

15.2 UPDATE WITH CONSTRAINTS

Consider a database system with constraints, and suppose the database system receives an update request that, if executed literally, would lead to a dataset that violates the constraints.

One course of action in this situation is for the system to simply reject the request, possibly with an indication of the possible problems (as suggested in the section on alerting in the unit on managing inconsistency).

An alternative is for the system to *repair* the update set by augmenting it with additions and deletions in such a way that the resulting update set leads to a dataset that reflects the requested updates *and* satisfies all constraints.

The bad news is that there is no method of repair that is satisfactory in all applications. The good news is that, using operation definitions, an administrator can specify how to make repairs in such situations.

As an example of this mechanism in action, consider the rules shown below. The first directs the system to remove a sentence of the form `male(X)` whenever the user adds a sentence of the form `female(X)` (in addition to adding `male(X)`). The second rule is analogous to the first with male and female reversed. Together, these two rules enforce the mutual exclusion on male and female.

```
add(female(X)) :: female(X) & ~male(X)
add(male(X)) :: male(X) & ~female(X)
```

Similarly, we can enforce an "inclusion dependency" on parent and adult by writing the following rule. If the user requests the system to add a sentence of the form parent(X,Y), then the system also adds a sentence of the form adult(X).

```
add(parent(X,Y)) :: adult(X)
```

Note that not all constraints can be enforced using update rules. For example, if a user suggests adding the sentence parent(art,art) to the database in our kinship example, there is nothing the system can do to repair this error; and, if it wants to maintain consistency, it must reject the update.

A separate problem arises when there are multiple possible repairs and none seems better than the others. For example, we might have a constraint saying that every person is either male or female. If the user specifies a person fact involving a new person but does not specify the gender of that person, there may be no way for the system to decide that gender for itself. In such cases, the system could reject the request; it could collect additional information; or it could make an arbitrary choice and allow the user to modify the dataset using additional updates.

15.3 MAINTAINING MATERIALIZED VIEWS

A *materialized view* is a defined relation that is stored explicitly in the database. The benefit of materializing views is that a system can simply look up answers to questions about the materialized view rather than having to compute answers from other stored relations. The downside is that we need to keep such relations up-to-date as changes are made to the underlying base relations. Operation definitions can help here by enabling automatic updates to materialized views.

Suppose, for example, we had a database with parent and male as base relations; suppose we were to define father as a view of parent and male: and suppose we were to materialize the father relation. Then we could write update rules to maintain this materialized view. According to the first rule below, the system should add a sentence of the form father(X,Y) whenever the user adds parent(X,Y) and male(X) is known to be true. The other rules cover the other cases.

```
add(parent(X,Y)) :: male(X) ==> father(X,Y) &
add(male(X)) :: parent(X,Y) ==> father(X,Y)
```

```
delete(parent(X,Y)) :: ~father(X,Y)
delete(male(X)) :: ~father(X,Y)
```

This approach works, but it can be a little tedious to write such update rules. Fortunately, there are some alternatives. (1) First of all, it is possible to build a program that *differentiates* view definitions and produces such operation definitions automatically. (2) Second, it is possible to build differential update processing of this sort directly into a system's update engine. In this second case, explicit operation definitions are unnecessary. However, they remain useful in explaining how the system processes update requests.

15.4 UPDATE THROUGH VIEWS

In the preceding section, we discussed the process of updating views as a result of changes to the base relations in a dataset. In this section, we discuss the reverse of this process, viz. updating base relations when given changes to views of those relations. This process is often called *update through views*.

Updating views given changes to base relations is simple because there is a functional relationship between the views and the base relations in terms of which they are defined. The challenge in update through views is that there may be many extensions of the base relations that give rise to the same view extension. As a result, a change to a view relation can sometimes be accomplished in various ways, i.e., the update can be ambiguous.

As an example, consider a deductive database in which we are storing the p relation and the q relation, and suppose we are given the following definition of the r in terms of p and q.

```
r(X) :- p(X)
r(X) :- q(X)
```

Suppose now that the user asks us to add the fact r(a). How should we modify our dataset so that this conclusion holds? Should we add p(a) or q(a) or both?

Of course, a system could simply reject an update in the face of ambiguity. But in some cases the programmer might prefer that the system make a choice and leave it to the user to correct that choice if it is in error.

The beauty of operation definitions is that they allow the programmer to specify which of various possible base relation updates is appropriate given a change to an update to the view relations in a logic program.

As an example, in the case mentioned above, the programmer might choose to record p(a) (e.g., if there are far more p objects than q objects). In this case, he could specify this policy by writing the following operation definition.

```
add(r(X)) :: ~q(X) ==> p(X)
```

15.5 EXERCISES

15.1. Let us assume that the `likes` relation is symmetric, i.e., if one person likes another, then the second person likes the first. Define the `add` and `delete` operations to update the `likes` relation in a way that enforces the symmetry.

15.2. Parenthood is an asymmetric relation. It is not possible for a person to be his own parent. Define the `add` operation in such a way that it enforces the asymmetry of `parent` when the user requests the addition of a `parent` fact.

15.3. Assume that the `q` relation is defined as shown below. Define `add` and `delete` to update the `r` relation properly when a user requests the system to add or delete a `p` or `q` factoid.

```
r(X,Y) :- p(X,Y) & ~q(Y,X)
```

15.4. Assume that the `t` relation is defined as shown below. Define `add` and `delete` to update the `t` relation properly when a user requests the system to add or delete a `p` or `q` factoid.

```
t(X,Y) :- p(X,Y)
t(X,Y) :- q(X,Y)
```

15.5. Given the view definition shown below, there are three general ways to update the `p` and `q` relations when given a request to add or delete an atom involving the `r` relation. Define `add` and `delete` for each of these possibilities.

```
r(X,Y) :- p(X,Y) & q(X,Y)
```

CHAPTER 16

Interactive Worksheets

16.1 INTERACTIVE WORKSHEETS

Interactive worksheets are a simple but powerful way for people to manage data and to solve data-related problems. Examples of interactive worksheets range from simple, single-user spreadsheets (such as the interactive grids of cells in systems like Numbers and Excel) to collaborative, multi-institutional planning and design tools.

The power and popularity of interactive worksheets stems from a combination of features.

1. Meaningful data display. Data is typically presented on worksheets in forms suited to the type of data involved—as tables, charts, graphs, and so forth.

2. Modifiability. Data can be directly modified by the user in what-you-see-is-what-you-get fashion. Importantly, data can be changed in whatever order suits the user.

3. Constraint checking. Data is automatically checked for completeness and consistency with static and dynamic constraints. Users are alerted to problems; and, where possible, they are given guidance in eliminating those problems.

4. Automatic computation of results. Consequences of acceptable changes are automatically computed, and the presentation is updated to reflect those consequences.

While these features can be used in many information management settings, they have special value in certain types of applications, e.g., configuration tasks (such as product configuration worksheets and academic program sheets), teaching (such as interactive exercises and simulated environments), online games (such as Chess, Checkers, Pentago), and so forth.

The process of implementing interactive worksheets using traditional programming technologies is time-consuming and expensive. The good news is that Logic Programming can dramatically simplify this process. Making it easier for developers to create and maintain worksheets. And in many cases making it possible for non-developers to do the same. Creating and maintaining worksheets can and should be "do it yourself" (DIY). Just as it is possible for users without programming expertise to create and manage traditional spreadsheets, it should be possible for users without traditional programming expertise to create and manage worksheets on their own.

In this chapter, we see some ways in which Logic Programming techniques can be used in creating interactive worksheets that operate in World Wide Web browsers. Although our discussion focusses on this one class of interactive worksheets, the techniques can easily be applied to building interactive worksheets in other technologies.

16.2 EXAMPLE

As an example of an interactive worksheet implemented as a web page, take a look at the academic program sheet shown in `http://logicprogramming.stanford.edu/chapters/demo.html`. This worksheet provides a means for a student to design a program of study that achieves his academic goals and at the same time meets the academic requirements of his university.

The worksheet includes a listing of courses available to the student. At the bottom on the left, there is a pie chart indicating the proportion of his selected courses in various subareas of Computer Science. In the middle, there is an indication of the number of units of credit the student is requesting for each selected course. And, on the right, there is a listing of professors responsible for those courses.

The student can change his program by selecting courses in whatever order he likes. Clicking an empty checkbox adds the corresponding course to his program of study. Clicking a checkbox that is already checked removes the corresponding course from his program. Once a course is selected, the student can change the number of units of credit for each course by using the slider associated with that course.

An important part of the update process is constraint checking. As each change is made, the worksheet checks that all academic requirements are satisfied. If there is a violation, the corresponding requirement turns red, indicating that there is something wrong. Once the requirement is satisfied once again, the requirement turns black.

As the program is modified, as changes are made, the worksheet is updated accordingly. For example, as each box is checked, it is added to the course list, and a photo of the associated professor appears. Moving the slider for a course changes the requested credit; and, as such changes are made, the pie chart automatically adjusts to show the portion of time the student is devoting to various subareas of the department.

This is a simple example, but it illustrates the key features of interactive worksheets—visibility of all relevant data, the ability to modify that data, automatic checking of constraints, and automatic calculation and display of consequences.

16.3 PAGE DATA

The data underlying a web page appearing in a browser typically takes the form of a hierarchical data structure called a *DOM* (short for *Document Object Model*). The top node in this data structure represents the document, and its child nodes represent its components. Nodes in the DOM typically have attributes of various sorts (e.g., the width and height of a table); and, in some cases, those attributes are objects with attributes of their own (e.g., the style attribute of a node has attributes of its own (e.g., font family, font size, and so forth).

In order to use Dynamic Logic Programming to specify the appearance and behavior of a web page, we need vocabulary to represent the state of a DOM in the form of factoids that express this state.

First of all, we assign identifiers for the nodes of the DOM that we care about. In order to give them meaning, we assign each of our identifiers as the value of the `id` attribute of the corresponding node. For example, if we wanted to use the identifier `mynode` to refer to the input element in the HTML fragment shown below, we would list that identifier as the `id` attribute of that input widget, as shown in this example.

```
<center>
  <input id='mynode' type='text' value='hello'
  size='30' style='color:black'/>
</center>
```

Next, we invent predicates to describe the various properties of these nodes. See below for the most commonly used predicates. For example, we use the binary predicate `value` to associate an input node (selector or type-in field or textarea) with its value.

`value(`***`widget`***`,`***`value`***`):`
: This factoid is true whenever the value associated with *widget* is *value*. The widget here may be a text field, selector, radio button field, slider, and so forth.

`holds(`***`widget`***`,`***`value`***`):`
: This factoid is true whenever one of the values associated with the multi-valued node *widget*. The widget in this case multi-valued selector or a checkbox field.

`attribute(`***`widget`***`,`***`property`***`,`***`value`***`):`
: This factoid is true whenever the *property* attribute of *widget* is *value*.

`style(`***`widget`***`,`***`property`***`,`***`value`***`):`
: This factoid is true whenever the *property* style of *widget* is *value*.

`innerhtml(`***`widget`***`,`***`content`***`):`
: This factoid is true whenever the *innerHTML* of *widget* is *content*. Note that *content* is typically a string of characters.

Given this vocabulary, we can encode relevant information in the form of a dataset. For example, the relevant state of the DOM fragment shown above can be represented by the dataset shown below.

```
value(mynode,hello)
attribute(mynode,size,30)
style(mynode,color,black)
```

16.4 GESTURES

User interaction with a web page takes the form of *gestures* (e.g., keystrokes and mouse-clicks). In order to talk about these gestures, we need appropriate vocabulary. For example, we use the constant `click` to represent the operation of clicking on a button. We use the constant `select` to represent the operation of selecting a specific option from a selector.

`select(`***`widget`***`,`***`value`***`):`
: This action occurs when the user enters or selects *value* as the value of *widget*. The widget here may be an object or text field, a selector, a multi-valued menu, a checkbox field, a radio button field, a slider, and so forth.

`deselect(`***`widget`***`,`***`value`***`):`
: This action occurs when the user erases or deselects *value* as the value of *widget*.

`click(`***`widget`***`):`
: This action occurs when the user clicks on *widget*.

`tick:`
: This action occurs periodically. By default, it happens once per second. It is also occurs the user clicks the Run button or the Step button in a simulation control box.

`load:`
: This occurs when a page is first loaded.

`unload:`
: This action occurs when a user leaves a page.

We use this vocabulary to represent user gestures. For example, if the user clicks a button with identifier `a`, we represent this as the action `click(a)`. If the user selects `3` from a selector with identifier `b`, we represent this as `select(b,3)`.

16.5 OPERATION DEFINITIONS

Given a vocabulary for encoding data and gestures, we can describe the behavior of a worksheet by writing suitable operation definitions. The following examples illustrate how this can be done.

Consider the following buttons with identifiers `orange`, `blue`, `purple`, and `black`.

orange blue purple black

Suppose that we wanted the worksheet to change the color of this document (identified as page) whenever the user clicks one of these buttons. This behavior can be described with the following operation rules.

```
click(orange) :: style(page,color,orange)
click(blue) :: style(page,color,blue)
click(purple) :: style(page,color,purple)
click(black) :: style(page,color,black)
```

Alternatively, we can write these rules more compactly by using a variable, as shown below.

```
click(X) :: style(page,color,X)
```

This rule reads as follows. If a user clicks on button with `X` as `id`, then, in the next state of the worksheet, the `color` style of the node identified as page should be `X`.

Although these operation rules work fine, they are not quite complete. This is because, after clicking the above buttons, the state of our worksheet may include more than one fact of the form `style(page,color,X)`. To completely specify the desired behavior, we need to remove the existing style factoids for page when a button is clicked. This can be done with the following operation rule.

```
click(X) :: style(page,color,Y) & distinct(X,Y) ==>
~style(page,color,Y)
```

This rule reads as follows. If a user clicks on button `X`, and the `color` of page is `Y`, and `Y` is different from `X`, then in the next state of the worksheet, the `color` of page should not be `Y`.

Now consider another example. Here we replace the four buttons with a selector with identifier `pagecolor` and four options `orange`, `blue`, `purple`, and `black`.

black

Let's suppose that we would like change the text color of this document based on the value selected. We can describe this behavior with the following rules.

```
select(pagecolor,X) :: style(page,color,X)
select(pagecolor,X) :: style(page,color,Y) ==> ~style(page,color,Y)
```

The first rule states that, if a user selects value `X` for `pagecolor`, then `style(page,color,X)` should be true in the next state, i.e., the text color of the page should be `X`. The second rule say that, if a user selects value `X` for `pagecolor` and the `style` of page is Y and Y is different from X, then style(page,color,X) should *not* be true in the next state.

Unfortunately, this is not quite enough. Our transition changes the color of the page, but there is nothing changing the value of the pagecolor attribute. As a result, it will reset to black after the gesture is processed. The following transition rules update the selector.

```
select(pagecolor,X) :: value(pagecolor,X)
select(pagecolor,X) :: value(pagecolor,Y) ==> ~value(pagecolor,Y)
```

As a final example, let's look at an example of interactions between input widgets. The operation rules for the four buttons in the first example change the color of the page correctly. However, they do not update the color indicated in the selector.

The transition rule shown below prescribes the desired behavior. When the user clicks a button with identifier X, then we want the value of the value of the selector to be updated and we want any previous value to be removed.

```
click(X) :: value(pagecolor,X)
click(X) :: value(pagecolor,Y) ==> ~value(pagecolor,Y)
```

Combining these rules with the rules shown above allows the user to click either the buttons or make selections and get the same effects in both cases.

16.6 VIEW DEFINITIONS

In the preceding section, we saw that a single gesture can have multiple effects. For example, changing the value of a selector named pagecolor sets the value of the selector *and* changes the color of the page. To implement this behavior, we need to manage both conditions in our transition rules, and we need to store both conditions in our dataset. Moreover, if we are not careful, our definitions might get out of sync with each other, and we would not get the behavior we want.

The good news is that it is sometimes possible to write *view definitions* that describe such behavior more economically and in a way that is less prone to mistakes. By defining some of our predicates as *views* of other predicates, we do not need to store as much information and we can get by with fewer transition rules.

In the case from the preceding section, suppose that we were to define the color of the page node in terms of the value of the pagecolor node. The definition is shown below.

```
style(page,color,X) :- value(pagecolor,X)
```

With this definition in place, we could replace the operation rules shown in the last section with the four shown below.

```
click(X) :: value(pagecolor,X)
click(X) :: value(pagecolor,Y) ==> ~value(pagecolor,Y)

select(pagecolor,X) :: value(pagecolor,X)
select(pagecolor,X) :: value(pagecolor,Y) ==> ~value(pagecolor,Y)
```

There are fewer rules here, and they mention fewer predicates. In particular, there is no mention of the style of the page. That property is fully determined by the value of `pagecolor`, and so we do not need to store or update this information in our rules. Instead, the worksheet computes the style using the view definition given above.

16.7 SEMANTIC MODELING

So far, we have talked about purely *reactive* worksheets—in which behavior is defined directly in terms of visible features and user gestures. In this section, we look at *semantic* modeling—where behavior is defined in terms of relationships among objects in the application area of the worksheet (e.g., people, places, movies, and so forth). We look at how we can use operation rules to update this semantic data, and we look at how we can use view definitions to define syntactic attributes in terms of semantic information.

Consider a course scheduling worksheet that is laid out as follows. In this layout, the multi-valued selectors have identifiers `course1`, `course2`, `course3`, and `course4`, and they have options `autumn`, `winter`, `spring`, and `summer`.

Course 1	Course 2	Course 3	Course 4
Autumn	Autumn	Autumn	Autumn
Winter	Winter	Winter	Winter
Spring	Spring	Spring	Spring
Summer	Summer	Summer	Summer

If a user of this worksheet selects the options `autumn` and `spring` in `course1`, then the factoids `holds(course1,autumn)` and `holds(course1,spring)` are added to our dataset. Semantically, this means that the user has selected `course1` for both the `autumn` and `spring` quarters.

Now, consider the alternative layout of this course scheduling worksheet shown below, where the selectors have identifiers `autumn`, `winter`, `spring`, and `summer` and where they have options `course1`, `course2`, `course3`, and `course4` (denoting the courses that may be taken in a quarter).

Autumn	Winter	Spring	Summer
Course 1	Course 1	Course 1	Course 1
Course 2	Course 2	Course 2	Course 2
Course 3	Course 3	Course 3	Course 3
Course 4	Course 4	Course 4	Course 4

In this alternative layout, the user's course selections correspond to the facts `holds(autumn,course1)` and `holds(spring,course1)`. Note that these facts are different from the ones stored in the previous worksheet, i.e., `holds(course1,autumn)` and `holds(course1,spring)`. However, at a conceptual level, nothing has changed! In both cases, the user has selected `course1` for both the `autumn` and `spring` quarters.

The difference between the states of these two conceptually identical worksheets is due to the difference in their layout. One way to design a semantic model of a worksheet is to separate out *what is stored* in a worksheet's state from *what is rendered*, e.g., `style`, `value`, `holds` facts.

The first step is to write out operation rules for the gestures on the worksheet's widgets and have the effects correspond to semantically meaningful relations.

For example, in the first course scheduling worksheet, we would use the operation rules shown below.

```
select(Course,Quarter) :: taken(Course,Quarter)
deselect(Course,Quarter) :: ~taken(Course,Quarter)
```

In the second course scheduling worksheet, which is conceptually identical to the first one, we would write the following rules.

```
select(Quarter,Course) :: taken(Course,Quarter)
deselect(Quarter,Course) :: ~taken(Course, Quarter)
```

The second step in creating a semantic worksheet is to define the layout of the worksheet as a view over these semantically meaningful relations.

For example, in the first course scheduling worksheet, we would define `holds` as a view of `taken`

```
holds(Course,Quarter) :- taken(Course,Quarter)
```

In the second course scheduling worksheet, we would define `holds` as shown below.

```
holds(Quarter,Course) :- taken(Course,Quarter)
```

Now, suppose a user selects `course1` in `autumn` and `spring` quarters. The facts stored in both worksheets would be identical.

```
taken(course1,autumn)
taken(course1,summer)
```

The upshot is that the rules on each sheet, in effect, constitute a *stylesheet* for displaying and updating that data. An important benefit of this is that the application data implicit in a worksheet can be exchanged with other worksheets that manage the data in different ways.

PART V

Conclusion

CHAPTER 17

Variations

17.1 INTRODUCTION

In this chapter, we give brief descriptions of a few additional types of Logic Programming: Logic Production Systems, Constraint Logic Programming, Disjunctive Logic Programming, Existential Logic Programming, Answer Set Programming, and Inductive Logic Programming.

17.2 LOGIC PRODUCTION SYSTEMS

Production systems are a programming language paradigm that has been widely used both for computer applications such as expert systems and for representing the processes involved in human thinking. Rules in a production system have the form: *conditions* → *actions*. The rules are executed in a *cycle*: facts in a *working memory* are matched with the conditions to derive the actions to be executed. A working memory is similar to a dataset considered in this volume. If more than one rule matches the conditions, a selection is performed to choose which rule should be executed. The execution of a rule involves adding and removing facts from the working memory. An example rule selection strategy is to associate priorities with the rules, and choose a higher priority rule over a lower priority rule. The repeated execution of the rules generates the successive states of the working memory, and this behavior provides an *operational semantics* to the rules.

Production rules have been used to model three kinds of situations: stimulus-response associations; forward chaining; and goal-reduction. We saw an example of a stimulus-response association in Section 14.2 in the system with three lights: whenever the user pushes a button, which is a stimulus, the response is for the system to toggle the corresponding light.

```
push_button :: p  ==> ~p
push_button :: ~p  ==> p
```

The following rule which we saw in Section 4.5 is an example of forward chaining, as any time we add a *parent* fact, new *grandparent* facts are derived and added to the dataset. Such rules can also be generalized as operations for updating materialized views as shown in Section 15.3.

```
parent(X,Y) & parent(Y,Z) ==> grandparent(X,Z)
```

As an example of goal reduction, and in the context of the planning problem considered in Section 11.4, consider the following rule in which we state that if our goal state can be achieved by performing an action a in state s, and it is possible for us to perform the action a in state s, then that goal can be reduced to the goal of achieving state s.

```
goal(do(a,s)) & possible(a,s)  ==>  goal(s)
```

From the above examples, we can see that a natural analog exists between production rules and dynamic rules and operations considered in this volume. In the Logic Production Systems (LPS) framework, the production rules of the first kind are represented as dynamic rules, and the production rules of the second and third kind are represented as view definitions. In addition to giving dynamic rules an operational semantics similar to that of production systems, LPS also gives dynamic rules a logical semantics. It interprets dynamic rules as declarative sentences that need to be made true in a model that contains a sequence of time-stamped relation values, external events, and actions.

17.3 CONSTRAINT LOGIC PROGRAMMING

Consider the Peano Arithmetic from Section 10.2, and the following query:

```
number(L) & number(M) & add(L,M,N) & add(L,M,s(N))
```

As the above query is equivalent to proving `N = N + 1`, it is trivially false, but when posed to a logic programming system, it will run indefinitely. This is because the evaluation algorithm considered in Chapter 8 does not check satisfaction of constraints across subgoals. In a constraint logic program (CLP), the set of all constraints are tested for satisfiability at each step in the evaluation, and therefore, it is able to answer that the above query is false.

In addition to checking global satisfaction of constraints, a CLP system allows constraints to be stated directly as equations; it allows constraints to appear in queries; and during the evaluation of the queries, it can generate new constraints. To illustrate these features, consider the following program that computes the sum `S` of integers from `0` to `N`:

```
sumto(0,0)
sumto(N,S) :- N ≥ 1 & N ≤ S & sumto(N-1,S-1)
```

In the second rule above, constraints are stated directly using equation terms, and arithmetic expressions appear as arguments to a subgoal. Furthermore, the second rule is unsafe because both `N` and `S` are used in its body before they are bound. A CLP system is able to handle such unsafe rules. It can also generate new constraints during the evaluation. For example, during the evaluation of the query, `S ≤ 1`, the second rule above will lead to the following expanded version of its body:

```
N = N₁ & S = S₁ & N₁ ≥ 1 & N₁ ≤ S₁ & sumto(N₁ -1,S₁-1)
```

The above examples illustrated the simplest form of constraints handled by the CLP systems: arithmetic equality and inequality. Such arithmetic constraints can appear in view definitions considered in this volume. We saw an example use of such arithmetic inequality constraints in the Cryptarithmetic problem in Section 6.5 even though the solution of that problem did not require checking constraints across subgoals. In a constraint logic programming framework, the unification procedure of Chapter 8 is generalized to invoke the constraint solver whenever the expressions to be matched contain constraints. At each step of the evaluation, we must find a unifier between the selected subgoal and the goal to be proven, and generate any new constraints. In addition, we must check the consistency of the current set of constraints with the constraints in the body of the view definition. Thus, two solvers are involved: unification, and the specific constraint solver for the constraints in use.

Numerous extensions to the basic framework of CLP exist for problems that go beyond simple arithmetic equality and inequality constraints. In some CLP systems, it is possible to allow constraints in which values are floating point numbers or are defined using polynomial equations. CLP has also been used for combinatorial search problems, for example, the Map Coloring problem from Chapter 3. In some combinatorial problems, the goal is to not just find one solution, but finding optimal solutions according to one or more optimization criteria; finding all solutions; replacing (some or all) constraints with preferences; and considering a distributed setting where constraints are distributed among several agents.

17.4 DISJUNCTIVE LOGIC PROGRAMMING

In Chapter 2, we defined a dataset as a collection of simple facts that characterize the state of an application area. Facts in a dataset are assumed to be true; facts that are not included in the dataset are assumed to be false. There are situations when our knowledge of the application domain is incomplete in that given a set of facts we know that one or more them must be true but we do not know which of them is true. For example, given a person object `joe`, we know that either of `male(joe)` or `female(joe)` must be true, but we may not know which of these is true.

To understand the difficulty posed by incomplete information, consider a world in which we have two objects `a` and `b`, a unary relation `p`, and a disjunctive sentence `(p(a) | p(b))` (where `|` is the *or* operator). Recall from Chapter 7 that a factoid is *logically entailed* by a closed logic program if and only if it is true in every model of the program. In this example, a set containing `p(a)`, a set containing `p(b)`, and a set containing both `p(a)` and `p(b)` are models of the program, but their intersection is empty, and therefore, the only model is the empty set. This allows us to conclude both `~p(a)` and `~p(b)` which contradicts our disjunctive sentence. There has been extensive research on disjunctive logic programming to investigate different techniques that allow us to reason effectively with such incompleteness. We consider one such technique next.

We compute a set of definite facts as those ground atomic facts that occur in all the minimal models or in none of the minimal models. If we need to determine whether (p(a) | p(b)) is true, it suffices to check if p(a) is true or if p(b) is true in every minimal model. If that is true, we can conclude that (p(a) | p(b)) is true. To better appreciate this technique, let us consider a more involved disjunctive logic program shown below.

```
q(a)
p(a) | p(b)
```

The above program has two minimal models: one containing q(a) and p(a), and the other containing q(a) and p(b). Here, the set of definite facts includes q(a) as it appears in both the minimal models, and it includes q(b) as it does not appear in any of the minimal models. We can establish the truth of p(a) | p(b) by verifying that each minimal model contains either p(a) or p(b).

17.5 EXISTENTIAL LOGIC PROGRAMMING

An existential rule is a rule that has an atom with a functional term in its head. Such rules are also known as tuple generating dependencies in database systems. For our purposes, a logic program that contains existential rules is referred to as an existential logic program. Consider the following existential rules.

```
owns(X,house(X)) :- instance_of(X,person)
has_parent(X,f(X)) :- instance_of(X,person)
has_parent(X,g(X)) :- instance_of(X,male)
instance_of(f(X),person) :- instance_of(X,person)
instance_of(g(X),person) :- instance_of(X,person)
```

The first rule asserts that if X is a person, then X owns house(X). The second rule asserts that if X is a person, then f(X) is the parent of that person. The third rule asserts that if X is a male, then g(X) is the parent of X. The fourth and fifth rules assert that for every person, f(X) and g(X) are also instances of a person. Each of these five rules has a functional term in its head, and is therefore, an existential rule.

Existential rules can be written in Basic Logic Programming, but their effective usage present two new challenges: termination of reasoning and reasoning with incomplete knowledge.

The first existential rule shown above is the simplest form of an existential rule; and, by itself, it does not present any problem with termination of reasoning. But, the fourth existential rule leads to a non-terminating behavior, because it can be recursively applied to itself, leading to infinitely many conclusions.

Let us next consider an example of incomplete knowledge. From the second rule, we conclude `has_parent(X,f(john))`, and from the third rule, we conclude `has_parent(X,g(john))`, but the relationship between `f(john)` and `g(john)` is underspecified. Logically, `f(john)` and `g(john)` are two separate objects, but there are situations when it may be desirable to conclude that they refer to the same person.

17.6 ANSWER SET PROGRAMMING

While defining the semantics of logic programs in Section 7.3, we said that an interpretation D satisfies a ground atom p if and only if p is in D. We further said that D satisfies a ground negation ~p if and only if p is *not* in D. This approach to defining the semantics is also known as *negation as failure*, because we assume a negated atom to be satisfied because of its absence in D. For a safe and stratified logic program, negation as failure semantics ensures that there is a unique model.

Answer Set Programming (ASP) is an approach for defining the semantics of logic programs that may not be stratified. For example, consider the following rules.

```
p(1)                p(2)                          p(3)
q(3) :- ~r(3)       r(X) :- p(X) & ~q(X)
```

The above rules are not stratified. In ASP, the above rules lead to two *answer sets* shown below.

Answer Set 1:

```
p(1)    p(2)    p(3)    q(3)    r(1)    r(2)
```

Answer Set 2:

```
p(1)    p(2)    p(3)    r(3)    r(1)    r(2)
```

An *answer set solver* is a program that takes an answer set program as an input and outputs all the answer sets of that program. A typical answer set solver does not require an input query. In this section, we consider the semantics of answer set logic programs, and some of their important extensions.

The first step in defining answer set semantics is to compute the set of all instances of our rules. For example, for the program considered above, the grounded program is shown below.

```
p(1)                         p(2)                          p(3)
q(3) :- ~r(3)                r(1) :- p(1) & ~q(1)
r(2) :- p(2) & ~q(2)         r(3) :- p(3) & ~q(3)
```

For a program that does not contain any negated atoms, or if it contains negated atoms but is safe and stratified, it will have exactly one answer set. The answer set of such a program is identical to its extension as defined in Section 7.3.

We next consider the programs that contain negated atoms which are not stratified. To decide whether a set S of ground atoms is an answer set, we form the *reduct* of the grounded program with respect to S, as follows. For every rule of the grounded program such that S does not contain any of the negated items in the body of the rule, we drop the negated atoms from that rule and only retain its positive atoms in the reduct. All other rules are dropped from the grounded program altogether. The reduct does not contain any negated atoms, and we compute its extension as defined in Section 7.3. If the extension coincides with S, then S is an answer set of the given program.

As an example, suppose we wish to test if S = {p(1), p(2), p(3)} is an answer set of the grounded program shown above. The reduct of the program with respect to S is shown below.

```
p(1)              p(2)              p(3)
q(3)              r(1) :- p(1)
r(2) :- p(2)      r(3) :- p(3)
```

The extension of the reduct is {p(1), p(2), p(3), r(1), r(2), r(3), q(3)} which is different from S. Hence, S = {p(1), p(2), p(3)} is not an answer set of this program.

Now, suppose S = {p(1), p(2), p(3), q(3), r(1), r(2)}. The reduct of the program with respect to this new answer set is shown below.

```
p(1)    p(2)            p(3)
q(3)    r(1) :- p(1)    r(2) :- p(2)
```

The extension of this program is {p(1), p(2), p(3), q(3), r(1), r(2)} which is identical to S. Hence S = {p(1), p(2), p(3), q(3), r(1), r(2)} is an answer set of this program.

Answer set semantics provides an elegant way to define the meaning of unstratified logic programs. ASP has been found to be a useful approach for declarative specification for a broad range of combinatorial problems especially the ones that involve specifying complex constraints. In addition, the ASP framework lends itself to easy generalization to deal with arithmetic and disjunction. Public domain and commercial ASP solvers are now available that have impressive run time performance on small problems.

17.7 INDUCTIVE LOGIC PROGRAMMING

Induction is reasoning from the specific to the general. For example, consider the following dataset on kinship that is similar to what we have considered in the earlier chapters.

```
parent(a,b)     parent(a,c)     parent(d,b)
father(a,b)     father(a,c)     mother(d,b)
male(a)         female(c)       female(d)
```

Given the above dataset, we can use inductive reasoning to infer the following rules (or view definitions):

```
father(X,Y) :- parent(X,Y) & male(X)
mother(X,Y) :- parent(X,Y) & female(X)
```

In Inductive Logic Programming, given a dataset, a set of starting view definitions, and a target predicate, we can infer a view definition for the target predicate. In the example above, we are given a dataset, no starting view definitions, and we can infer the view definition of `father` and `mother`.

In the context of the Inductive Logic Programming, the dataset is also referred to as a set of positive examples. Some inductive reasoning algorithms also take as input a set of negative examples. If negative examples are not provided, they can be computed as the set of ground atoms in the Herbrand base that are not present in the dataset. The combined set of positive and negative examples taken together is also known as training data.

There are two broad classes of Inductive Logic Programming algorithms: top down, and inverse deduction. In a top down approach to learning, we start with a general view definition, and we restrict it until it satisfies all the positive and negative examples. In the inverse deduction approach, we start from the known facts, and we search for view definitions that would have been necessary to derive those facts.

APPENDIX A

Predefined Concepts in EpilogJS

A.1 INTRODUCTION

EpilogJS is a library of Javascript subroutines designing for processing logic programs written in Epilog. This appendix is a user guide for the predefined functions, the predefined relations, and the various operators supported by EpilogJS.

A.2 RELATIONS

`same(`***`expression,expression`***`)`
: The sentence `same(`x`,`y`)` is true if and only if x and y are identical. For example, `same(f(b),f(b))` is true.

`distinct(`***`expression,expression`***`)`
: The sentence `distinct(`x`,`y`)` is true if and only if x and y are *not* identical. For example, `same(f(a),f(b))` is true.

`evaluate(`***`expression,expression`***`)`
: The sentence `evaluate(`x`,`y`)` is true if and only if the value of x is y. For example, `evaluate(plus(2,3),5)` is true.

`member(`***`expression,list`***`)`
: The sentence `member(`x`,`l`)` is true if and only if x is a member of the list l. For example, `member(b,[a,b,c])` is true.

`true(`***`sentence,expression`***`)`
: The sentence `true(`p`,`d`)` is true if and only if the sentence p is true in the dataset named d. For example, if the dataset named `mydataset` contains the sentence `p(a,b)`, then `true(p(a,b),mydataset)` is true.

A.3 MATH FUNCTIONS

`abs(number)` → *`number`*

The value of `abs(x)` is the absolute value of x. For example, the value of `abs(-8)` is 8.

`acos(number)` → *`number`*

The value of `acos(x)` is the inverse cosine of x. For example, the value of `acos(1)` is 0.

`acosh(number)` → *`number`*

The value of `acosh(x)` is the inverse hyperbolic cosine of x. For example, the value of `acosh(1)` is 0.

`asin(number)` → *`number`*

The value of `asin(x)` is the inverse sine of x. For example, the value of `asin(0)` is 0.

`asinh(number)` → *`number`*

The value of `asinh(x)` is the inverse hyperbolic sine of x. For example, the value of `asinh(0)` is 0.

`atan(number)` → *`number`*

The value of `atan(x)` is the inverse tangent of x. For example, the value of `atan(0)` is 0.

`atan2(number,number)` → *`number`*

The value of `atan2(x,y)` is the inverse tangent of x/y. For example, the value of `atan2(0,1)` is 0.

`atanh(number)` → *`number`*

The value of `atanh(x)` is the inverse hyperbolic tangent of x. For example, the value of `atanh(0)` is 0.

`cbrt(number)` → *`number`*

The value of `cbrt(x)` is the cube root of x. For example, the value of `cbrt(8)` is 2.

`ceil(number)` → *`number`*

The value of `ceil(x)` is the smallest integer that is greater than x. For example, the value of `cbrt(2.2)` is 3.

`clz32(number)` → *`number`*

The value of `clz32(x)` is the number of leading zeros in the 32-bit representation of x. For example, the value of `clz32(2147483647)` is 1.

`cos(number)` → *`number`*

The value of `cos(x)` is the cosine of x. For example, the value of `cos(0)` is 1.

`cosh(`*`number`*`)` → *`number`*

The value of `cosh(`*x*`)` is the hyperbolic cosine of *x*. For example, the value of `cosh(0)` is `1`.

`exp(`*`number`*`)` → *`number`*

The value of `exp(`*x*`)` is *e* to the power of *x*. For example, the value of `exp(1)` is `~2.718281828459045`.

`expm1(`*`number`*`)` → *`number`*

The value of `expm1(`*x*`)` is *e* to the power of *x* minus 1. For example, the value of `expm1(0)` is `1`.

`floor(`*`number`*`)` → *`number`*

The value of `floor(`*x*`)` is *e* is the largest integer less than *x*. For example, the value of `floor(1.6)` is `1`.

`fround(`*`number`*`)` → *`number`*

The value of `fround(`*x*`)` is the nearest single precision floating point number to *x*.

`hypot(`*`number`*`,...,`*`number`*`)` → *`number`*

The value of `hypot(`*x1*`,...,`*xk*`)` is square root of the sum of the squares of *x1,...,xk*. For example, the value of `hypot(3,4)` is `5`.

`imul(`*`number`*`,`*`number`*`)` → *`number`*

The value of `imul(`*x*`,`*y*`)` is the product of *x* and *y* as though they were 32 bit signed integers. For example, the value of `imul(4294967295,-5)` is `5`.

`log(`*`number`*`)` → *`number`*

The value of `log(`*x*`)` is natural logarithm of *x*. For example, the value of `log(1)` is `0`.

`log1p(`*`number`*`)` → *`number`*

The value of `log1p(`*x*`)` is natural logarithm of *x*+1. For example, the value of `log1p(0)` is `0`.

`log2(`*`number`*`)` → *`number`*

The value of `log2(`*x*`)` is base 2 logarithm of *x*. For example, the value of `log(8)` is `3`.

`log10(`*`number`*`)` → *`number`*

The value of `log10(`*x*`)` is base 10 logarithm of *x*. For example, the value of `log(100)` is `2`.

`max(`*`number`*`,...,`*`number`*`)` → *`number`*

The value of `max(`*x1*`,...,`*xk*`)` is the maximum of *x1,...,xk*. For example, the value of `max(3,4,1,2)` is `4`.

`min(`*number*`,...,`*number*`)` → *number*

The value of `min(`*x1*`,...,`*xk*`)` is the minimum of *x1*,...,*xk*. For example, the value of `min(3,4,1,2)` is 1.

`minus(`*number*`,...,`*number*`)` → *number*

The value of `minus(`*x1*`,...,`*xk*`)` is the difference of *x1*,..., *xk*. For example, the value of `minus(9,4,3)` is 2.

`plus(`*number*`,...,`*number*`)` → *number*

The value of `plus(`*x1*`,...,`*xk*`)` is the sum of *x1*,..., *xk*. For example, the value of `plus(2,3,4)` is 9.

`pow(`*number*`,`*number*`)` → *number*

The value of `pow(`*x*`,`*y*`)` is *x* raised to the power *y*. For example, the value of `pow(2,3)` is `8`.

`quotient(`*number*`,...,`*number*`)` → *number*

The value of `quotient(`*x1*`,...,`*xk*`)` is the quotient of *x1*,..., *xk*. For example, the value of `quotient(12,3,2)` is 2.

`random()` → *number*

The value of `random()` is a random number between 0 (inclusive) and 1 (exclusive). For example, one possible value of `random` is `0.23`.

`round(`*number*`)` → *number*

The value of `round(`*x*`)` is *x* rounded to the nearest integer. For example, the value of `1.6` is 2.

`sin(`*number*`)` → *number*

The value of `sin(`*x*`)` is the sine of *x*. For example, the value of `sin(0)` is `0`.

`sinh(`*number*`)` → *number*

The value of `sin(`*x*`)` is the hyperbolic sine of i>x. For example, the value of `sinh(0)` is `0`.

`sqrt(`*number*`)` → *number*

The value of `sqrt(`*x*`)` is the positive square root of *x*. Works for any non-negative number *x*. For example, the value of 4 is 2.

`tan(`*number*`)` → *number*

The value of `tan(`*x*`)` is the tangent of *x*. For example, the value of `tan(0)` is `0`.

`tanh(`*number*`)` → *number*

The value of `tan(`*x*`)` is the hyperbolic tangent of *x*. For example, the value of `tanh(0)` is `0`.

times(*number,...,number*) → *number*

The value of times(*x*1,...,*xk*) is the product of *x1*,..., *xk*. For example, the value of times(2,3,4) is 24.

trunc(*number*) → *number*

The value of trunc(*x*) is the integer part of *x* (removing any fractional component. For example, the value of trunc(2.3) is 2, and the value of trunc(-2.3) is -2.

A.4 STRING FUNCTIONS

stringappend(*string,...,string*) → *string*

The value of stringappend(*s*1,...,*sk*) is the concatenation of s1, ..., sk. For example, the value of stringappend("Hello",",","World","!") is "Hello, World!".

stringmin(*string,...,string*) → *string*

The value of stringmin(*s*1,...,*sk*) is the *si* that is lexicographically smallest among the specified strings. For example, the value of stringmin("def","abc","efg") is "abc".

matches(*string,...,string*) → *string*

If the string *str* matches the regular expression *pat*, the value of matches(*str*,*pat*) is the list consisting of the substring of *str* that matches *pat* and the substrings of *str* that match the parenthesized components of *pat*. For example, the value of matches("321-1245","(.)-(.)") is ["1-1","1","1"].

submatches(*string,...,string*) → *string*

The value of submatches(*str*,*pat*) is the a list of all substrings of *str* that match the regular expression *pat*. For example, the value of matches("321-1245",".2.") is ["321","124"].

A.5 LIST FUNCTIONS

append(*list,...,list*) → *list*

The value of append(*l*1,...,*lk*) is the concatenation of l1, ..., lk. For example, the value of append([a,b,c],[d,e,f]) is [a,b,c,d,e,f].

revappend(*string,string*) → *string*

The value of revappend(*l*1,*l*2) is the result of concatenating the reverse of *x* onto *y*. For example, the value of revappend([a,b,c],[d,e,f]) is [c,b,a,d,e,f].

reverse(*list*) → *list*

The value of reverse([*x*1,...,*xk*]) is [*xk*,...,*x1*]. For example, the value of reverse([a,b,c]) is [c,b,a].

`length(list)` → *numbmer*
The value of `length(l)` is length of *l*. For example, the value of `length([a,b,c])` is 3.

A.6 ARITHMETIC LIST FUNCTIONS

`maximum([number,...,number])` → *number*
The value of `maximum([x1,...,xk])` is the maximum element in the specified list. For example, the value of `maximum([3,4,1,2])` is 4.

`minimum(list)` → *list*
The value of `minimum([x1,...,xk])` is the minimum element in the specified list. For example, the value of `minimum([3,4,1,2])` is 1.

`sum(list)` → *number*
The value of `sum([x1,...,xk])` is the sum of the elements in the specified list. For example, the value of `sum([3,4,1,2])` is 10.

`range(list)` → *number*
The value of `range([x1,...,xk])` is the range of the elements in the specified list, i.e., the difference between the maximum element and the minimum element. For example, the value of `midrange([3,4,2,1])` is 3.

`midrange(list)` → *number*
The value of `range([x1,...,xk])` is the midrange of the elements in the specified list, i.e., one half of the sum of the maximum element and the minimum element. For example, the value of `midrange([3,4,2,1])` is 2.5.

`mean(list)` → *number*
The value of `mean([x1,...,xk])` is the mean of the elements in the specified list. For example, the value of `mean([3,4,2])` is 3.

`median(list)` → *number*
The value of `median([x1,...,xk])` is the median of the elements in the specified list. For example, the value of `median([3,14,2])` is 3.

`variance(list)` → *number*
The value of `variance([x1,...,xk])` is the mean of the elements in the specified list. For example, the value of `variance([3,4,2,1])` is 1.25.

`stddev(list)` → *number*
The value of `stddev([x1,...,xk])` is the standard deviation of the elements in the specified list. For example, the value of `stddev([3,4,2,1])` is ~1.118033988749895.

A.7 CONVERSION FUNCTIONS

`symbolize(string)` → ***symbol***

The value of `symbolize(`*`str`*`)` is the symbol consisting of only the letters, underscores, and digits in *str* in which all uppercase letters have been converted to lowercase. For example, the value of `symbolize("Your name.")` is `yourname`.

`newsymbolize(string)` → ***newsymbol***

The value of `newsymbolize(`*`str`*`)` is the symbol consisting of only the letters, underscores, and digits in *str* in which all uppercase letters have been converted to lowercase and all spaces have been replaced by underscores. For example, the value of `newsymbolize("Your name.")` is `your_name`.

`readstring(string)` → ***expression***

The value of `readstring(`*`str`*`)` is first expression that can be parsed from the characters in *str*. For example, the value of `readstring("p(a) p(b)")` is `p(a)`.

`readstringall(string)` → ***expression***

The value of `readstring(`*`str`*`)` is the list of all expressions that can be parsed from the characters in *str*. For example, the value of `readstring("p(a) p(b)")` is `[p(a), p(b)]`.

`stringify(expression)` → ***string***

The value of `stringify(`*`expression`*`)` is string representation of *expression*. For example, the value of `stringify(p(a) & p(b))` is `"p(a) & p(b)"`.

`stringifyall(expression*)` → ***string***

The value of `stringifyall([`*x*`1,...,`*x*`l])` is string representation of *x1,...,xl*. For example, the value of `stringifyall([p(a), p(b)])` is `"p(a) p(b)"`.

`listify(expression)` → ***list***

The value of `listify(`*`expression`*`)` is the representation of *expression* as a list. For example, the value of `listify(p(a,b))` is `[p,a,b]`.

`delistify(list)` → ***expression***

The value of `delistify(`*l*`)` is the representation of *l* as an expression. For example, the value of `delistify([p,a,b])` is `p(a,b)`.

A.8 AGGREGATES

`setofall(expression,sentence)` → ***list***

The value of `setofall([`*x*`,`*p*`])` is the list consisting of all distinct instances of *x* for which the corresponding instance of *p* is true. For example, given a dataset containing `p(a,b)`, `p(a,c)`, and `p(a,d)`, the value of `setofall(X,p(a,X))` is `[b,c,d]`.

`countofall(`*`expression,sentence`*`)` → *`number`*

The value of `countofall([`x`,`p`])` is the number of distinct instances of x for which the corresponding instance of p is true. For example, given a dataset containing `p(a,b)`, `p(a,c)`, and `p(a,d)`, the value of `countofall(X,p(a,X))` is 3.

A.9 OPERATORS

`nil` The symbol `nil` is another representation for the empty list, i.e., `nil` and `[]` are synonymous.

`cons(`*`expression,list`*`)`

The symbol cons is the primary operator used in Epilog lists. For example, the list `[a,b,c]` is equivalent to `cons(a,cons(b,cons(c,nil)))`. Note that `a!b!c!nil` is another way of writing this expression.

`not(`*`sentence`*`)`

The symbol `not` is the primary operator in negations. For example the `~p(a)` is equivalent to `not(p(a))`.

`and(`*`expression,...,expression`*`)`

The symbol and is the primary operator in conjunctions. For example, `(p(X) & q(X))` is equivalent to `and(p(X),q(X))`.

`or(`*`expression,...,expression`*`)`

The symbol or is the primary operator in disjunctions. For example, `(p(X) | q(X))` is equivalent to `or(p(X),q(X))`.

`rule(`*`expression,...,expression`*`)`

The symbol `rule` is the primary operator of rules in view definitions. For example, the rule `r(X) :- p(X) & q(X)` is equivalent to `rule(r(X),p(X),q(X))`.

`definition(`*`expression,expression`*`)`

The symbol `definition` is the primary operator of function definitions. For example, the definition `f(X) := g(h(X))` is equivalent to `definition(f(X),g(h(X)))`.

`transition(`*`expression,expression`*`)`

The symbol `transition` is the primary operator of transition rules. For example, the transition rule `p(X) ==> q(X)` is equivalent to `transition(p(X),q(X))`.

`if(`*`condition1, expression1, ..., conditionN, expressionN`*`)`

The symbol `if` is the primary conditional operator in function definitions. The value of `if(condition1, expression1, condition2, expression2, ..., conditionN, expressionN)` is `expression1` is `condition1` is true, else `expression2` if `condition2` is true ... else `expressionN` if `conditionN` is true. For example, the value of `if(p(a),"yes",true,"no")` if `"yes"` if `p(a)` is true else `"no"`.

This builtin is a *variadic*, i.e., the number of arguments is not fixed.

`choose(`*`expression1, sentence`*`)`

The value of `choose(`*`expression, sentence`*`)` is a random member of the set `{`*`expression`*` | `*`sentence`*` evaluates to true}`. For example, for the dataset {`r(a)`, `r(b)`}, the value of `choose(f(X), r(X))` may either be `f(a)` or `f(b)`.

APPENDIX B

Sierra

B.1 INTRODUCTION

Sierra is a browser-based interactive development environment (IDE) for Epilog. It allows users to view and edit datasets and rulesets. It provides a variety of tools for querying and modifying datasets and rulesets. As changes are made, it automatically updates visible datasets in spreadsheet-like fashion in accordance with the user's rules. It also provides tools for analyzing datasets and rulesets, tools for tracing program execution, and tools for saving and loading files.

This document provides an introductory tour of the main features of Sierra. We see how to load Sierra; we see how to create, view, and edit datasets and rulesets; and we see how to save one's work for later use. We suggest repeating the steps shown here in one's browser as we proceed through the tour.

B.2 GETTING STARTED

Since Sierra is browser-based, we start by loading a suitable browser. (Sierra runs in Safari, Chrome, Firefox, and other browsers. In our examples here, we use Safari, although the appearance and interaction are virtually the same in all major browsers.)

`http://epilog.stanford.edu/homepage/sierra.php`

This brings up a page that looks like the following.

The command bar across the top provides access to menus concerning files, datasets, channels, rulesets, tools of various sorts, and system settings. We will introduce these menus one by one as we proceed with our tour.

B.3 DATA

Clicking on the Datasets menu, we see two choices—Lambda (the default dataset) and New Dataset (which is used to create additional named datasets). Let's start by clicking on Lambda. This opens a window showing the contents of the dataset named lambda. It is initially empty.

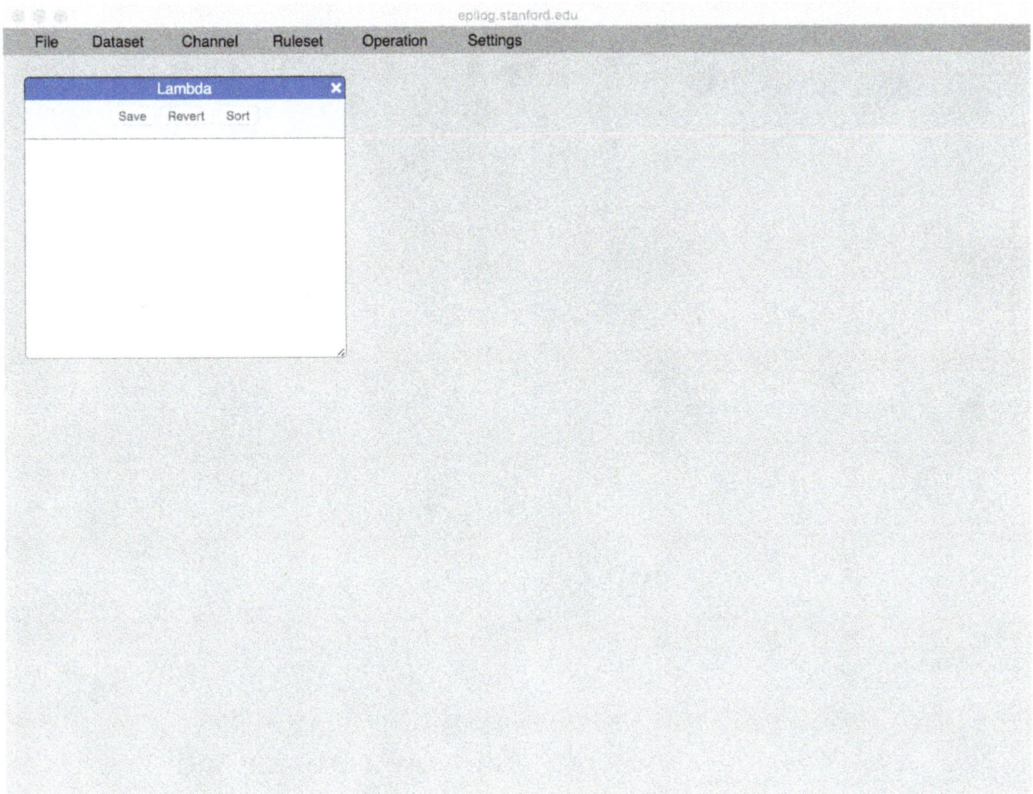

We can add data by typing into the window. Here we have entered the facts `p(c,d)`, `p(a,b)`, and `p(b,c)`. The window is highlighted in red indicating that we have made changes but not yet committed those changes to the database.

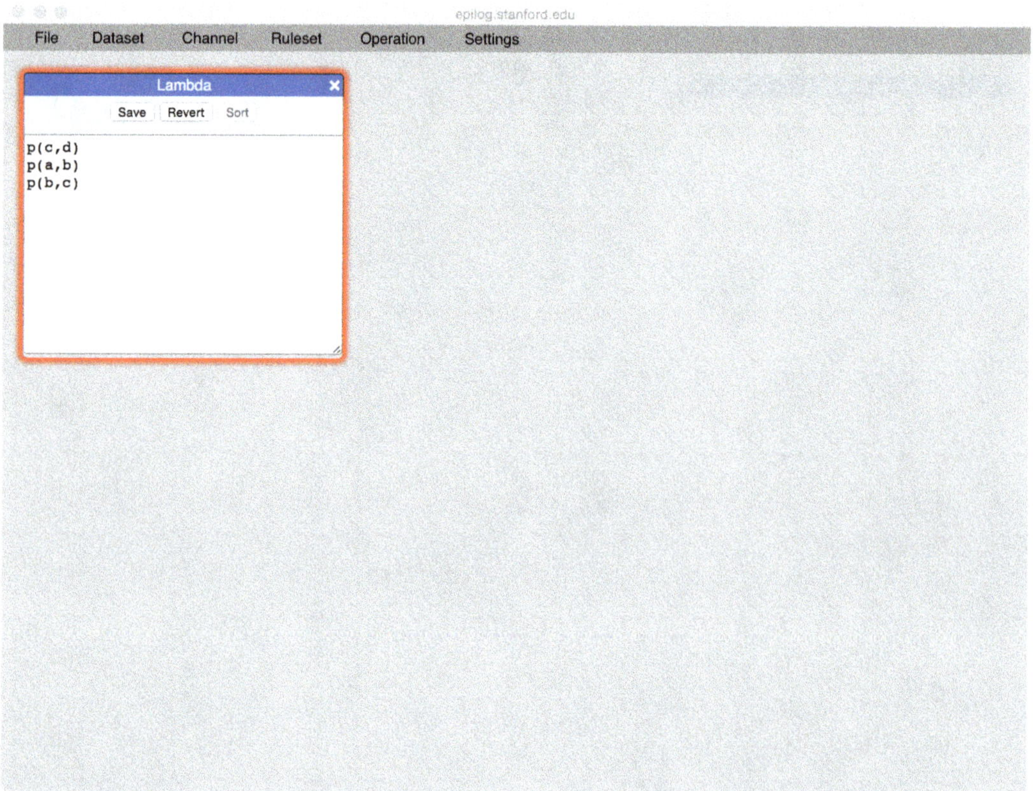

Clicking the save button stores the data and removes the highlighting, indicating that the window is showing the current data.

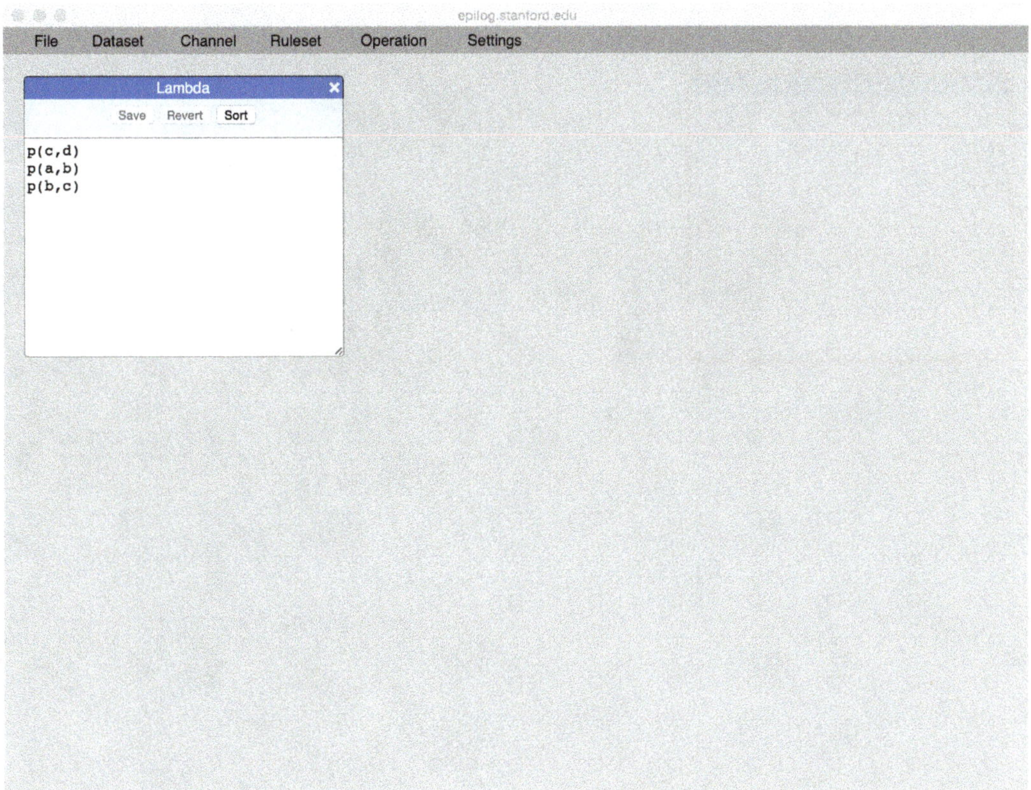

At this point, we can add or delete data or change it in other ways. One useful feature is sorting the data. This can be accomplished by pressing the Sort button. Note that the window is once again highlighted, indicating that the result of the sorting operation has not been saved to the database.

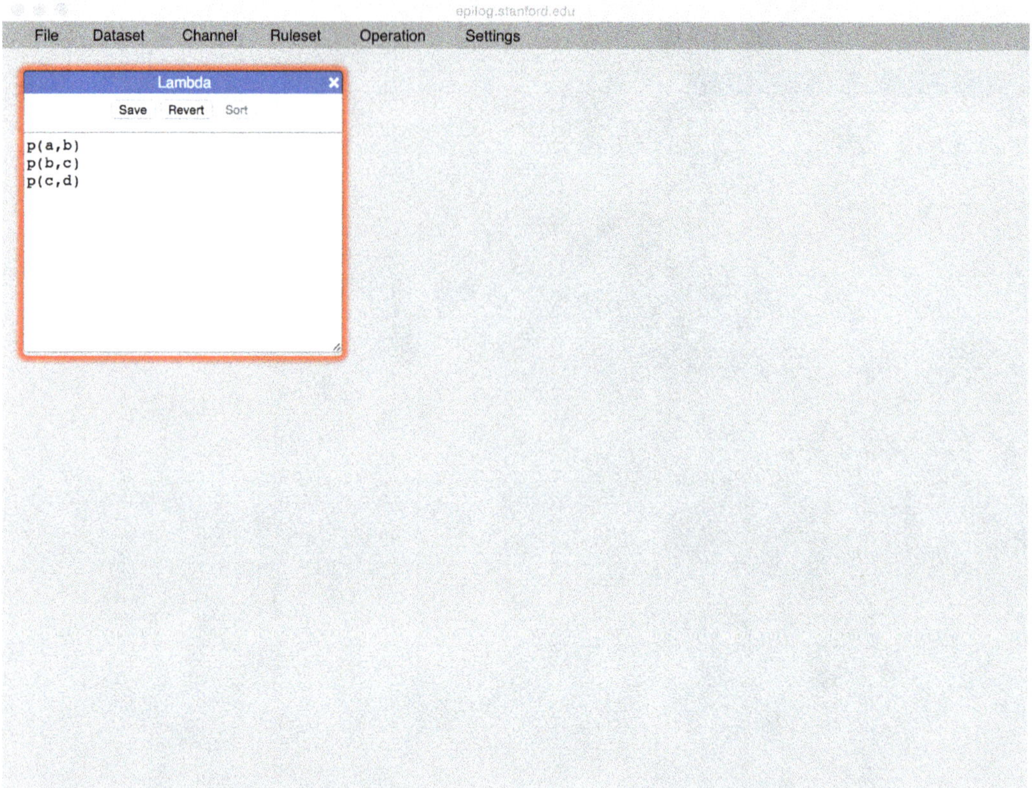

Pressing Save once again commits these changes to the database.

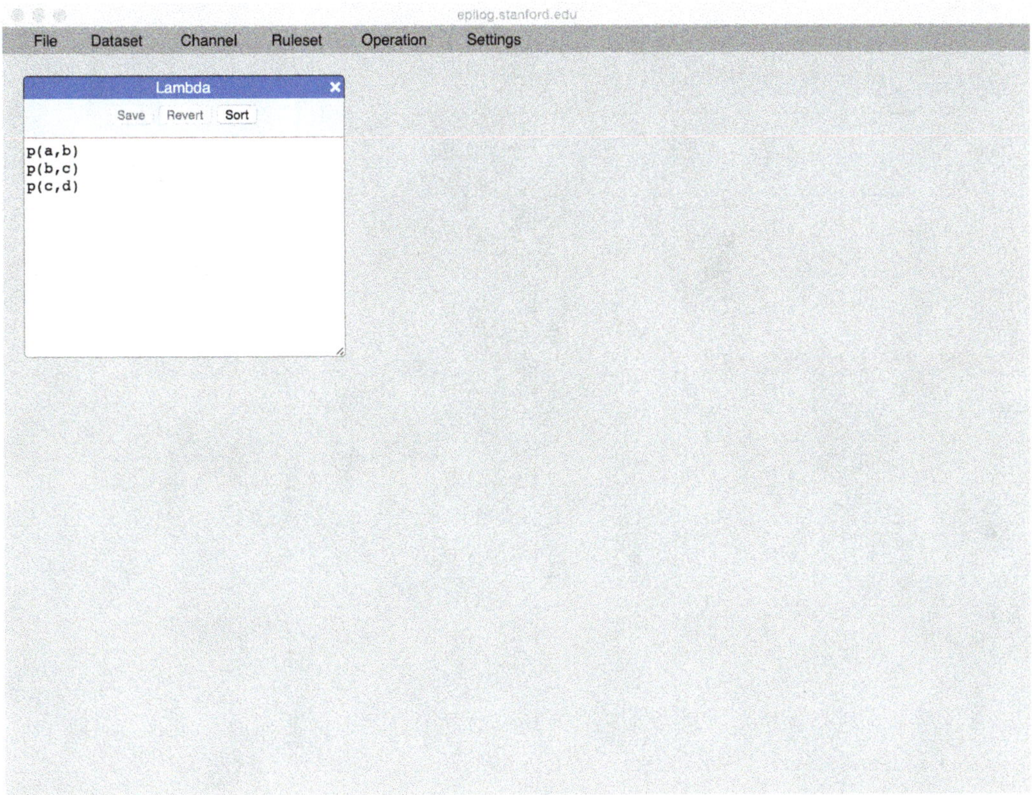

Suppose we edit the data and the result is syntactically illegal, as shown below.

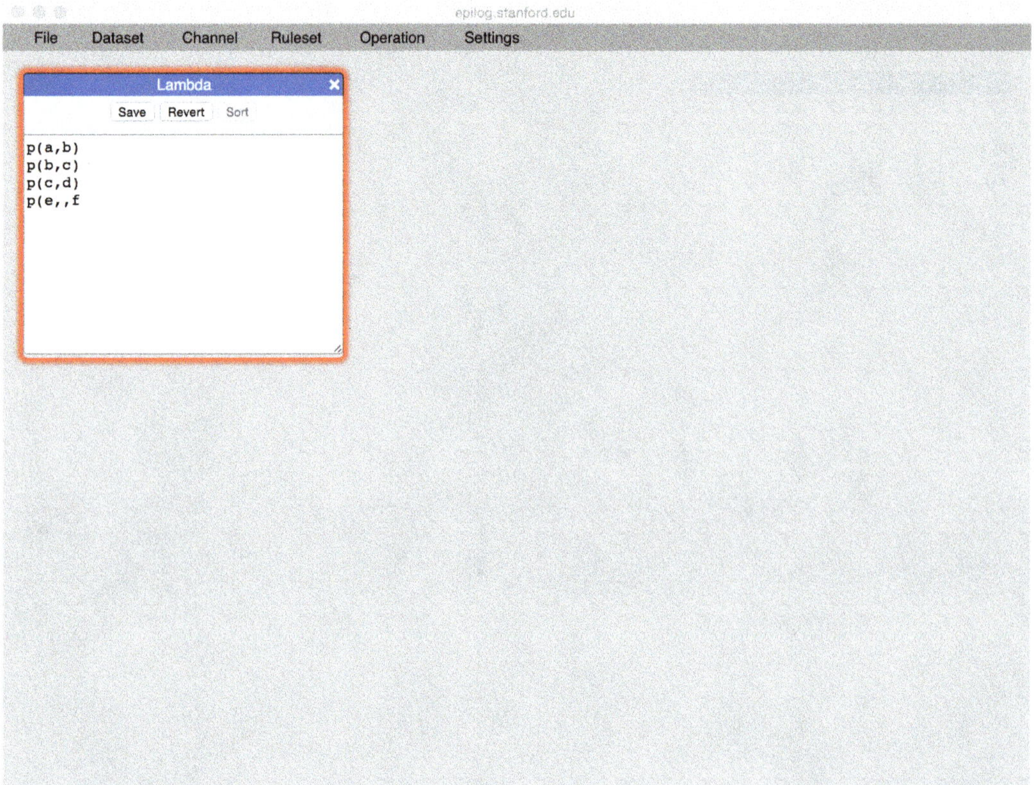

If we try to save the window, we will get an error message like the following, and the database will not be modified.

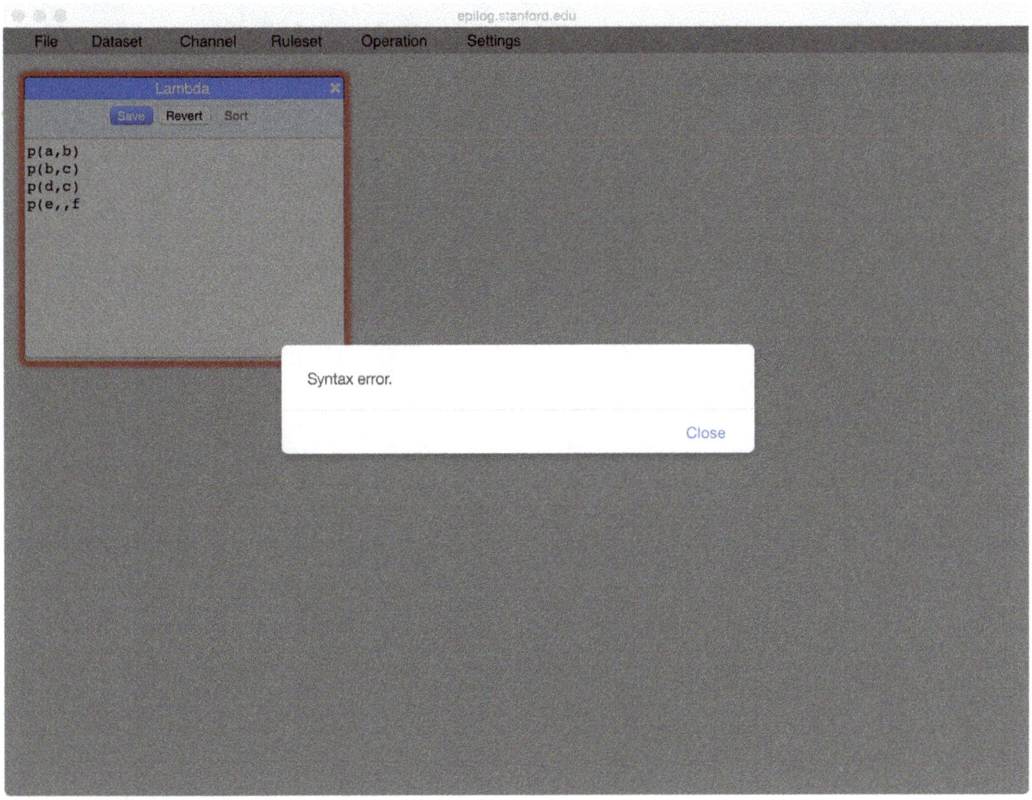

At this point, we can either repair the problem and try again, or we can click Revert to return to the current state of the dataset in the database, as we have done here.

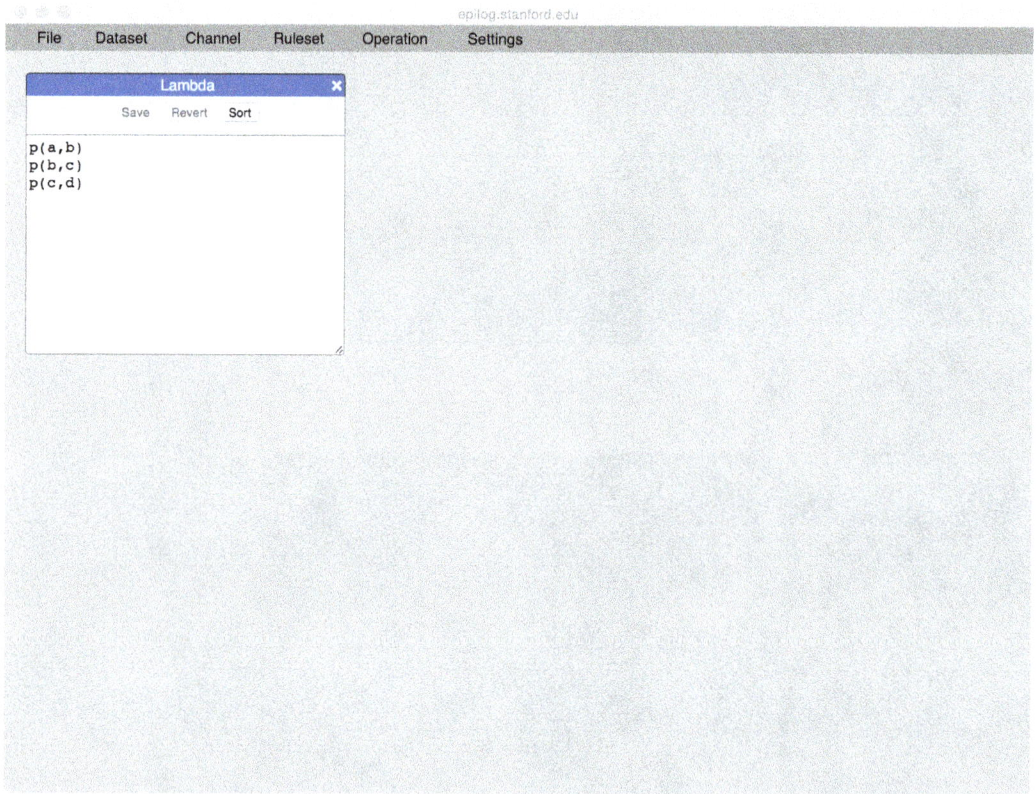

B.4 QUERIES

The Tools menu contains tools for programmatically querying and updating data. If we select the Query tool, we get a window like the one shown here. Note that the window may appear on top of an existing window. To move a window, we click on the title bar of the window and drag to the desired location. If we want to resize a window, we click on the tab in the lower right-hand corner and drag to the desired size. Here, we have repositioned the window to the right of lambda.

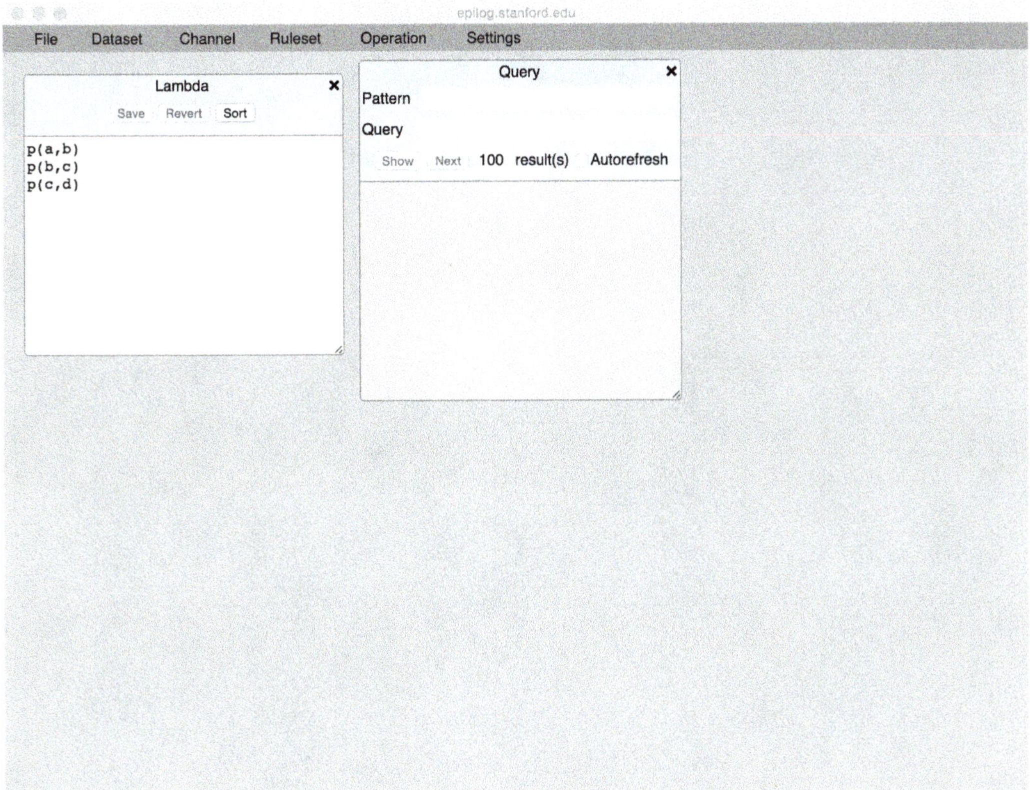

To form a query, we enter an expression for our desired answer in the Pattern field and we enter our query in the Query field. Here, we are asking for all expressions of the form `goal(X,Z)` where `p(X,Y) & p(Y,Z)` is true.

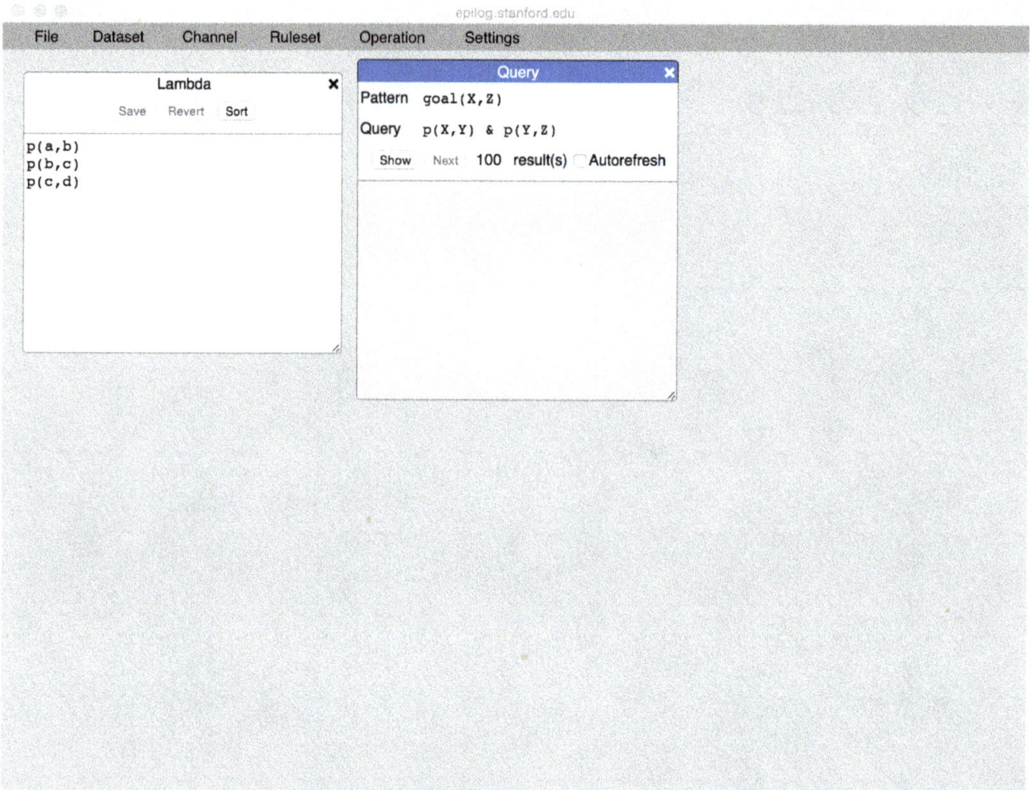

Pressing the Show button evaluates the query and places the results in the query window. In this case, there are just two answers, viz. `goal(a,c)` and `goal(b,d)`.

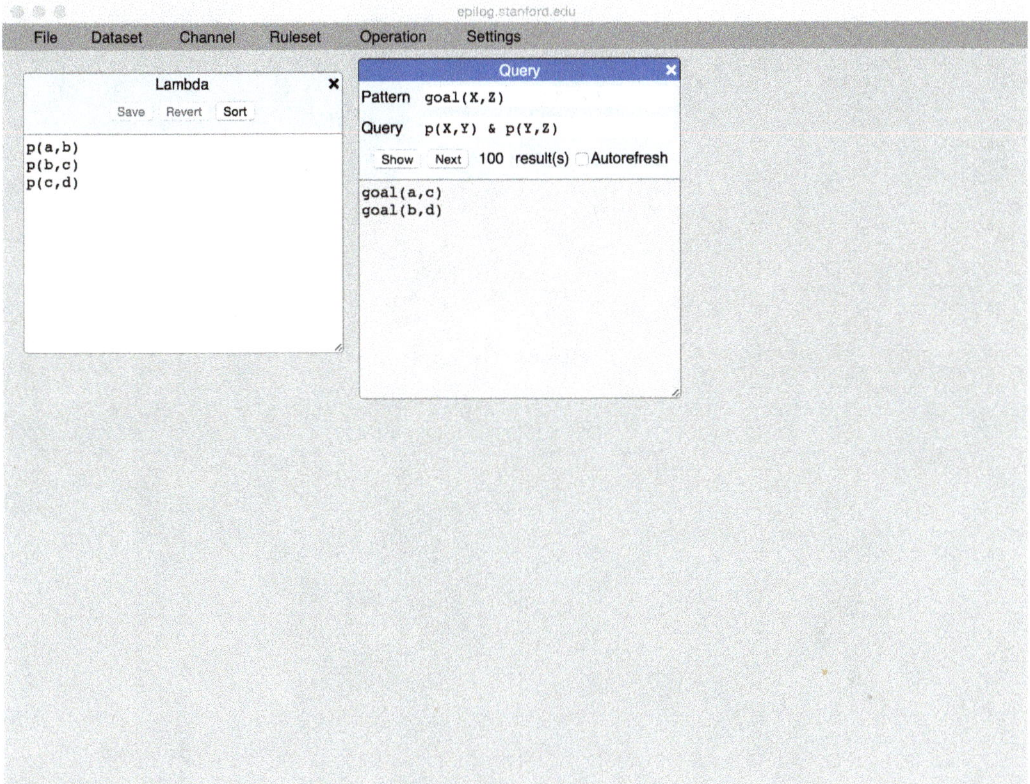

In general, queries can have many answers. By default, the Query tool shows only 100 answers, as shown in the count field. We can change this default by editing this field. In the case of expensive queries, it is often desirable to ask for just one result. Once a result or results have been shown, we can get the next batch of answers by clicking the Next button.

The Autorefresh checkbox tells the system whether we want the query to be recomputed automatically in responses to changes in the database and rulebase. Here, we have checked the box, thereby commanding automatic refresh.

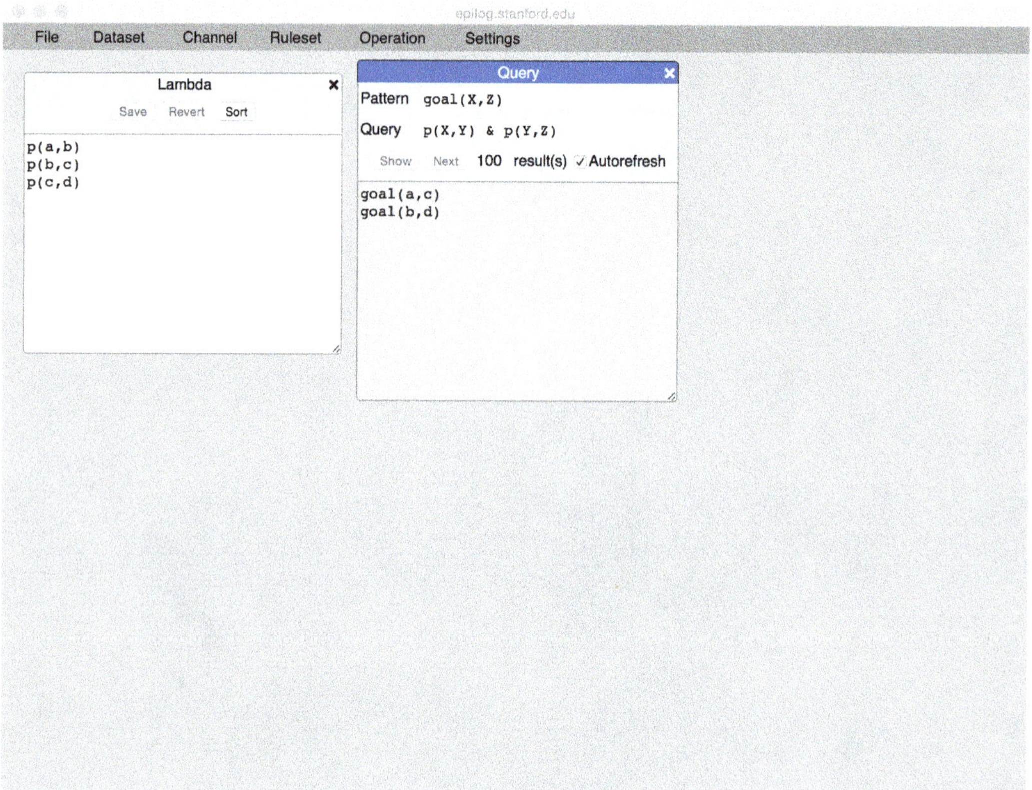

Now, let's go back to lambda and add another another fact.

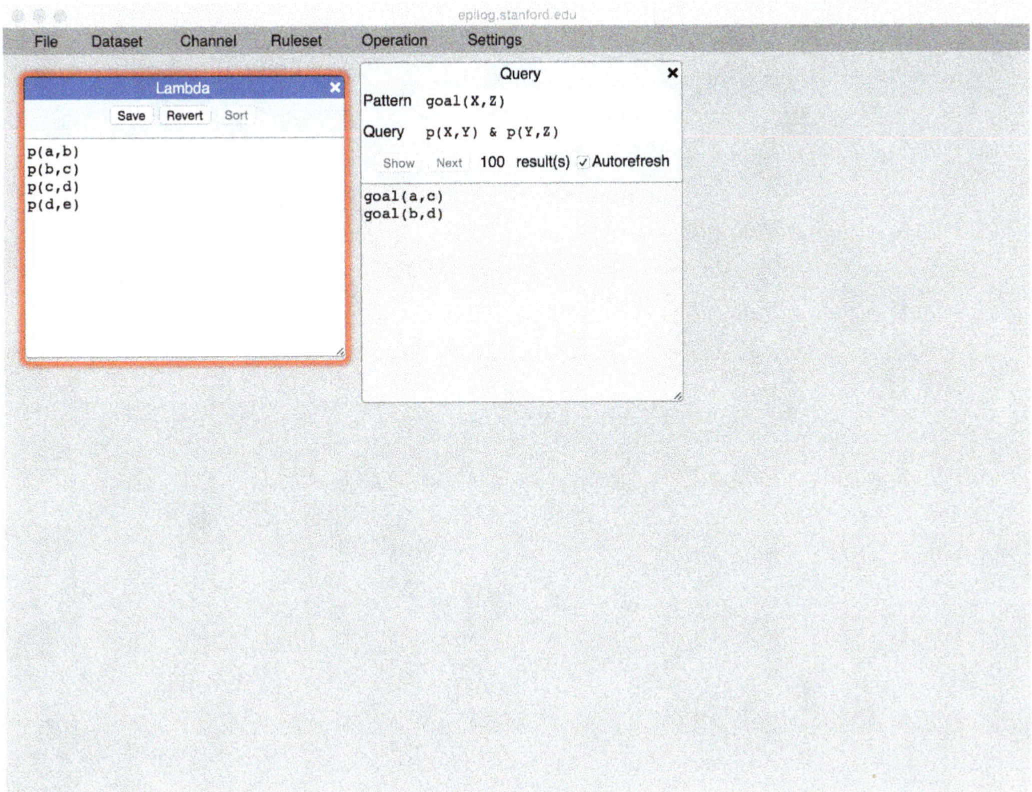

When we press Save, the data is saved and the Query window is automatically updated, as shown here.

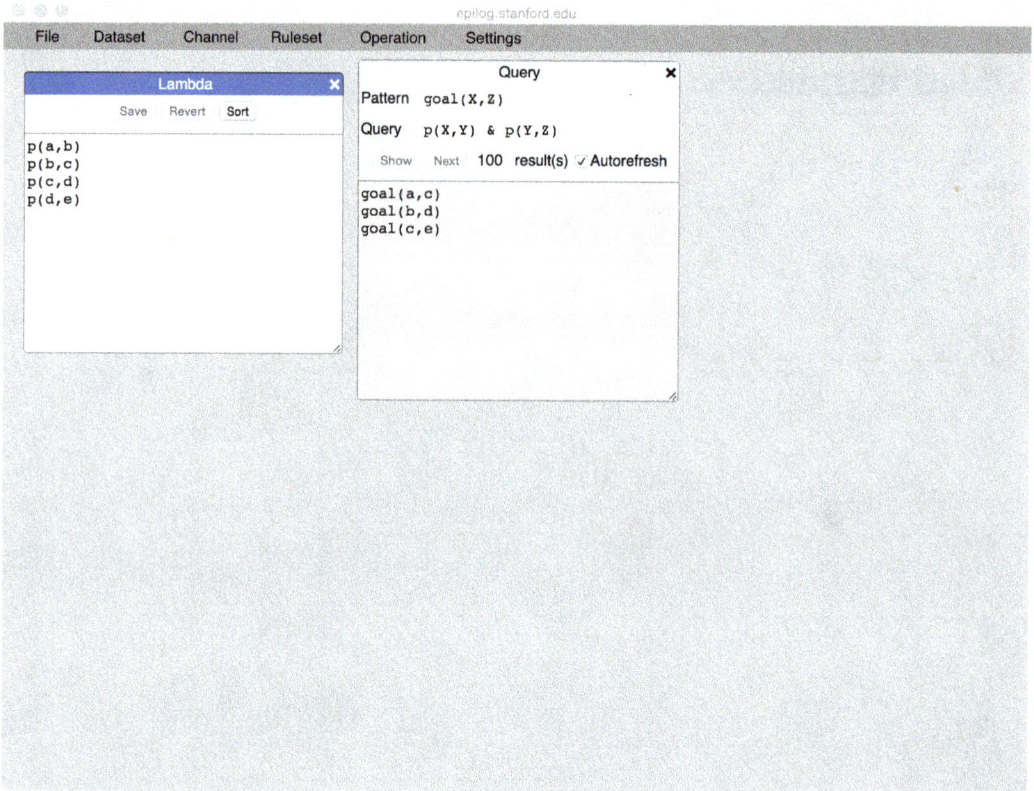

Note that it is common for users to have multiple query windows open at the same time and to have their Autorefresh boxes checked. When changes are made to the database, all such boxes are refreshed automatically in spreadsheet style.

B.5 UPDATES

The Tools menu also contains tools for programmatically modifying the database. Clicking on the Transform produces a window like the one shown here.

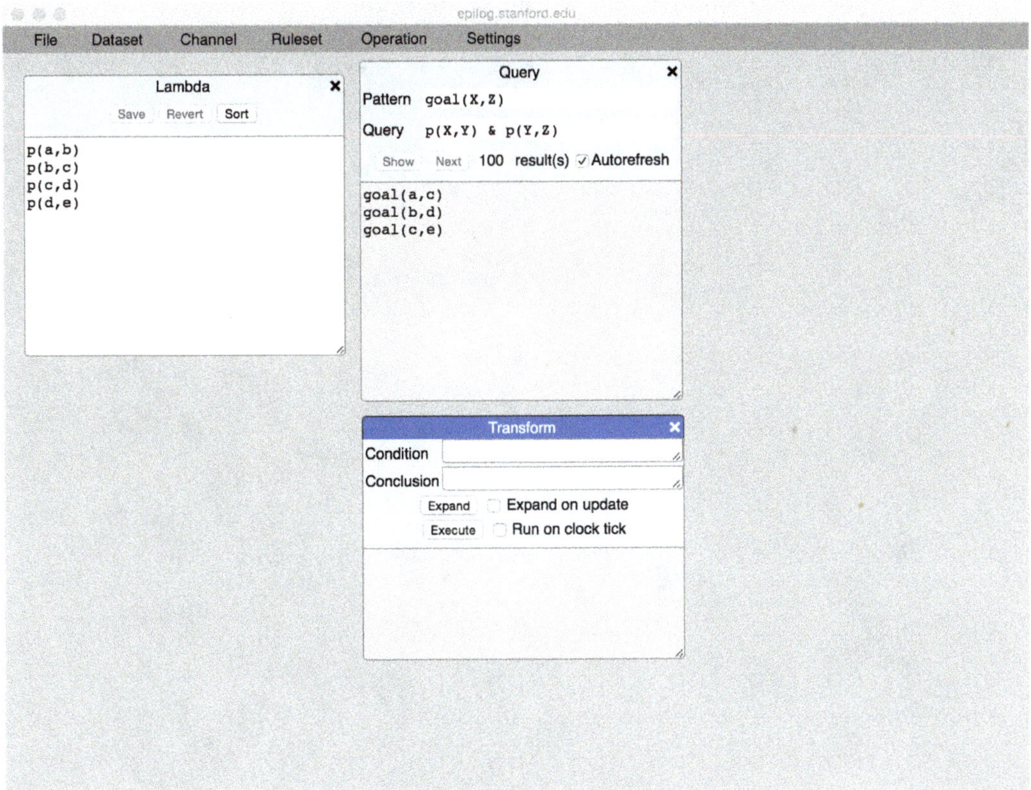

This tool allows us to perform transformations on the database. To specify a transformation, we enter a pattern into the Condition filed and a pattern in the Conclusion field, as shown here.

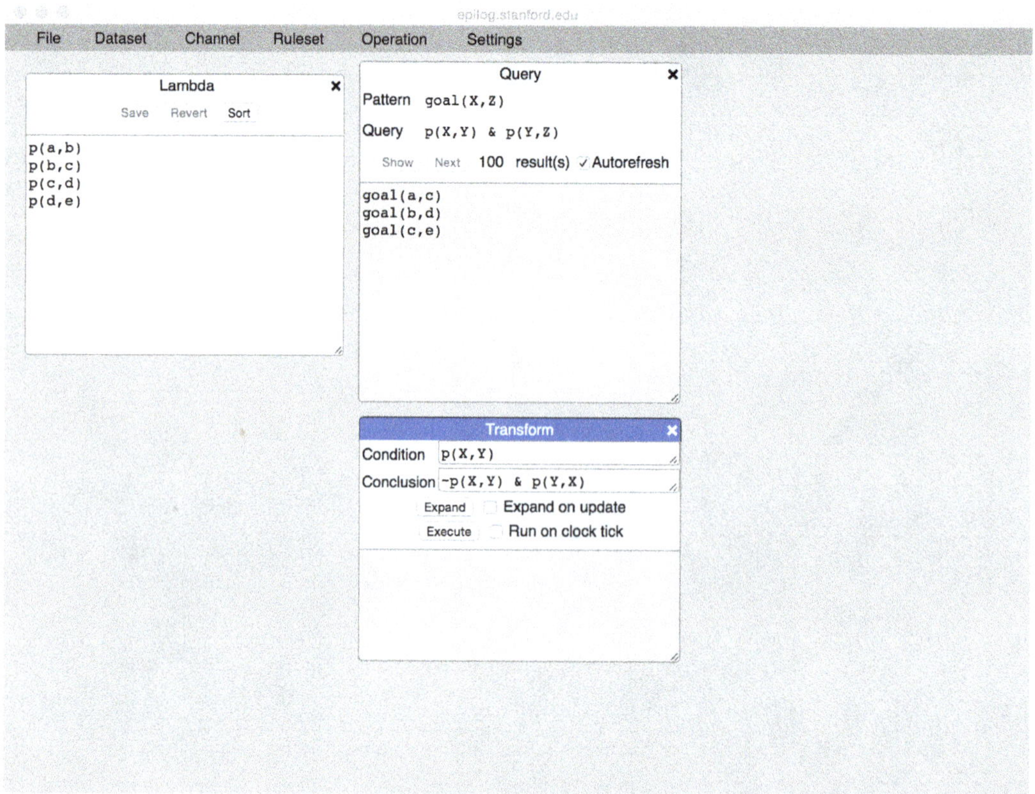

In executing a transformation, Sierra finds all variable bindings that satisfy the specified condition and, for each, modifies the database in accordance with the instances of the conclusion corresponding tho that variable binding. In this case, we are requesting that Sierra find all facts of the form `p(X,Y)`; and, for each of these, we want it to delete that fact and replace it with a fact of the form `p(Y,X)`, i.e., the same fact with the arguments reversed.

Pressing the Execute button in this case leads to the situation show below. Note that the facts in lambda have been changed as directed. Note also that the query window has been updated to reflect the new data.

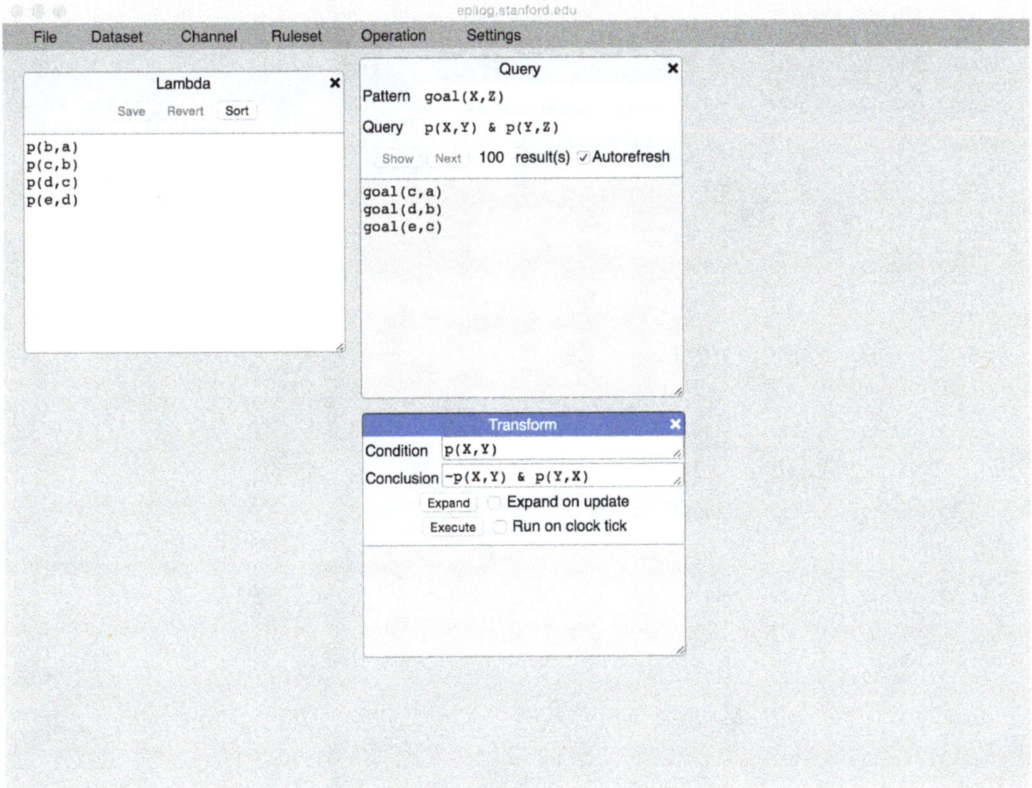

The Expand button asks Sierra to display the additions and deletions that would be performed if the transformation were to be executed in the current state. It is extremely useful in debugging to see changes before they are made.

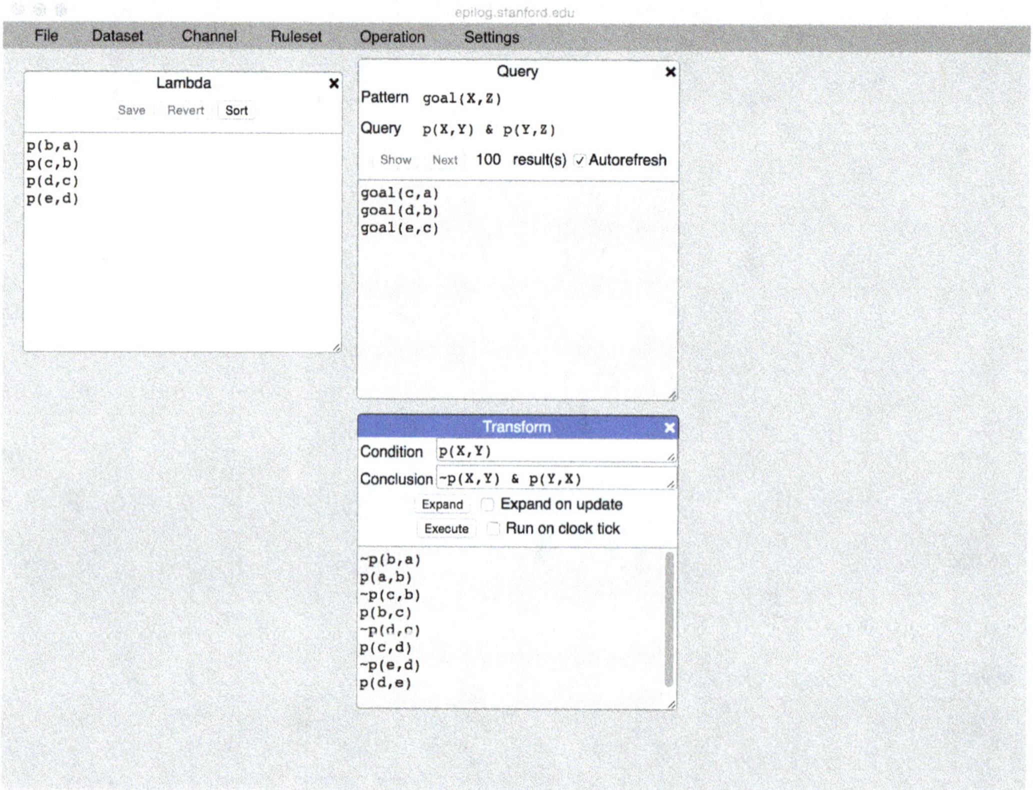

The Expand on Update checkbox directs Sierra to refresh the changes that would be necessary as the database changes. For example, if we were to check this box and click Execute, we would see the database switch back to its original state and display a different set of changes.

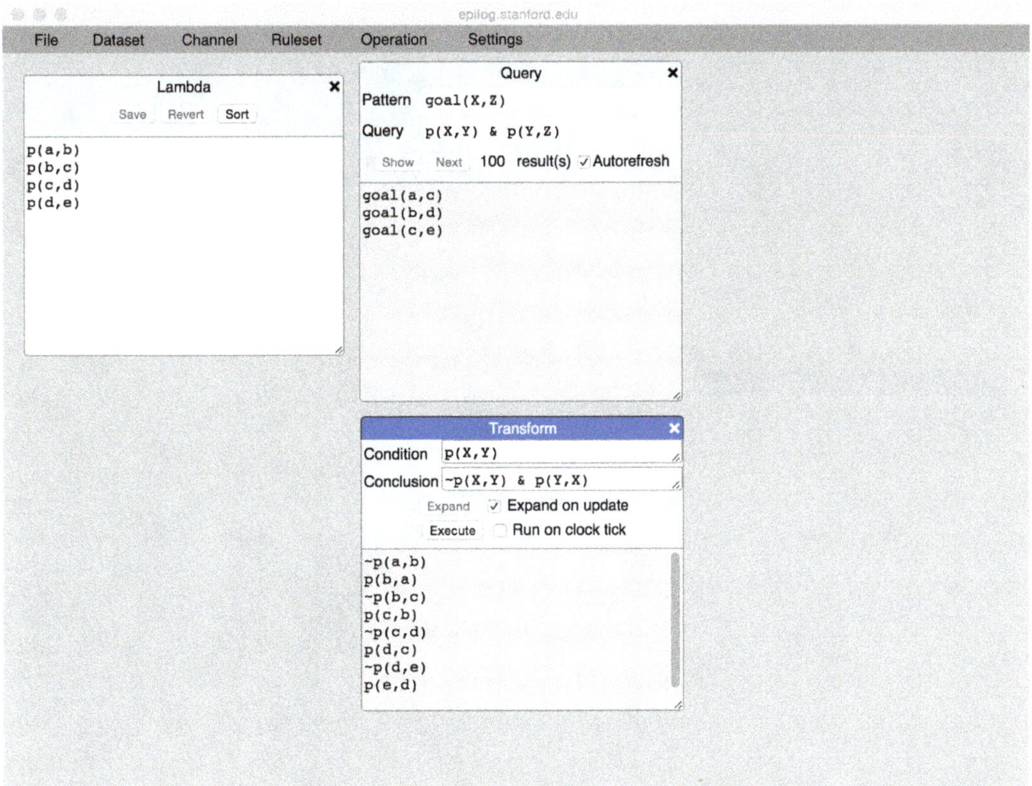

Finally, the checkbox labeled Run on Clock Tick allows us to schedule the transformation rule to run whenever the clock ticks. In this case, it would result in the order of arguments of the facts in the dataset oscillating back and forth. This case is not too interesting, but updating on clock tick is often useful in simulating dynamic systems.

B.6 VIEW DEFINITIONS

Views in Logic Programming are effectively named queries. An important benefit of this is composition. Once we have a name for a view, we can use that name in defining other views. Moreover, we can use the name in defining the view itself, i.e., in defining recursive views. View definitions are expressed by adding rules to a ruleset. In Sierra, rulesets are accessed via the Ruleset menu.

Clicking on the Ruleset menu, we see only one choice—Library. This is the default ruleset. (In advanced versions of Sierra, it is possible to manage multiple rulesets, but this feature is not enabled in the basic version shown here.)

Let's start by clicking on Library. This opens a window showing the contents of the ruleset named library. As with the lambda dataset, it is initially empty.

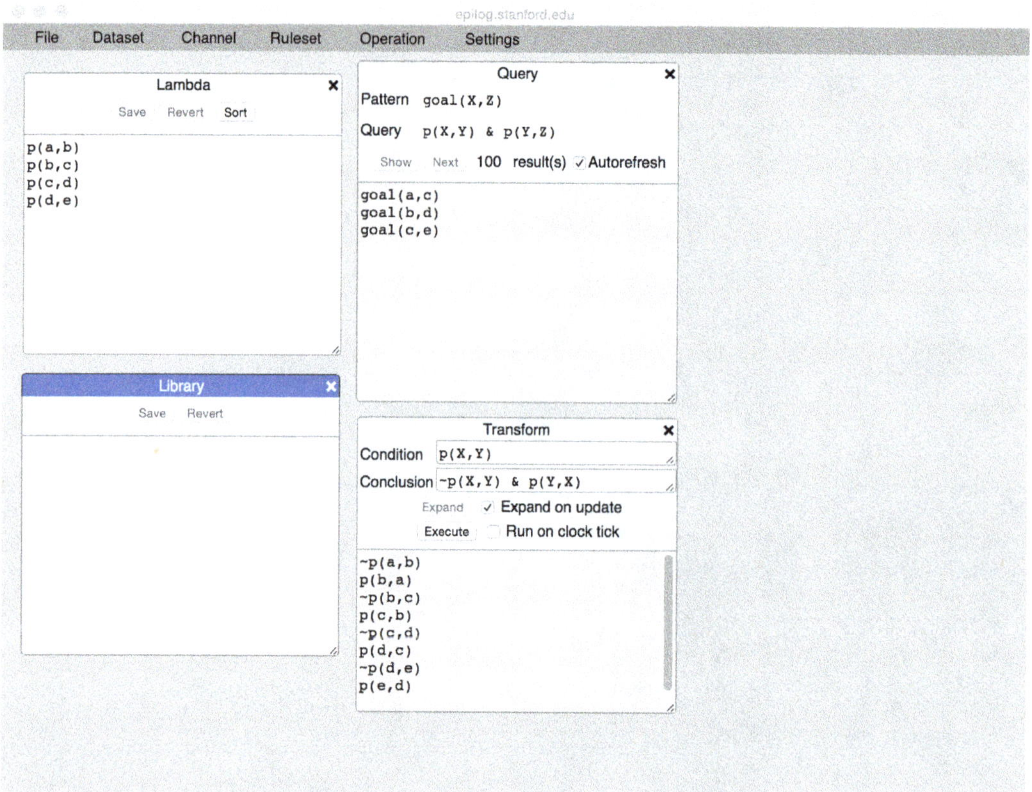

As this is a rule window, we can enter rules by typing in the window. Here, for example, we have defined the ancestor relation anc in terms of the parent relation p.

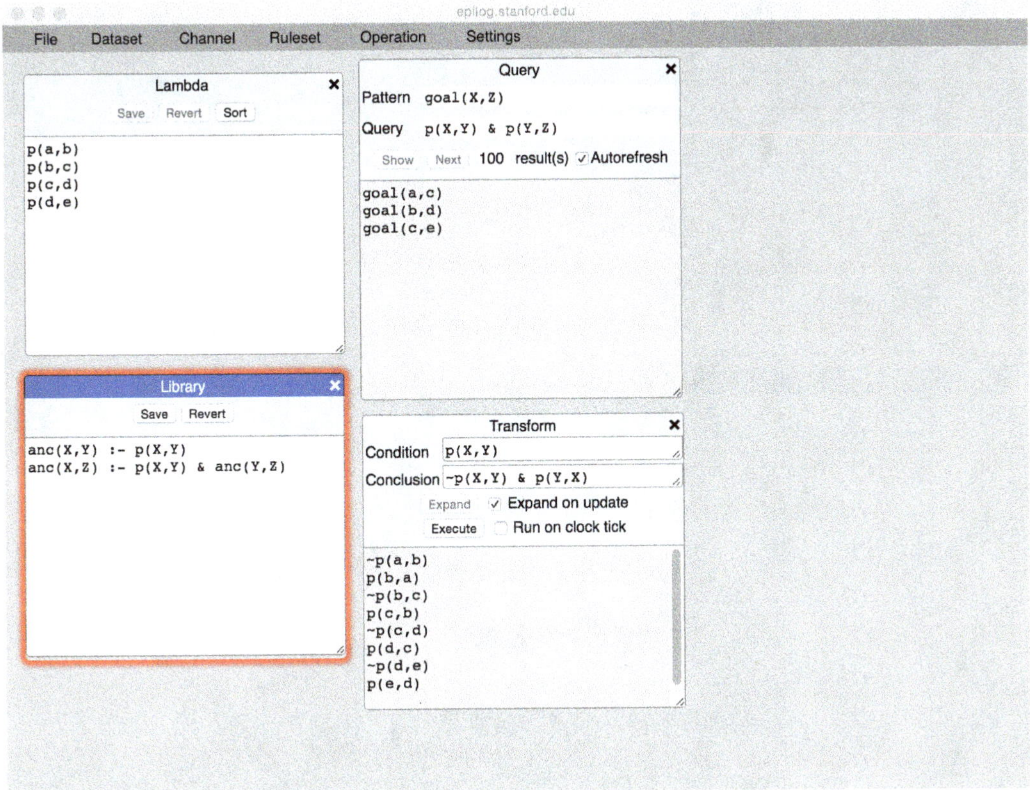

As with lambda, we need to click the Save button in order for our definition to be recorded in our ruleset.

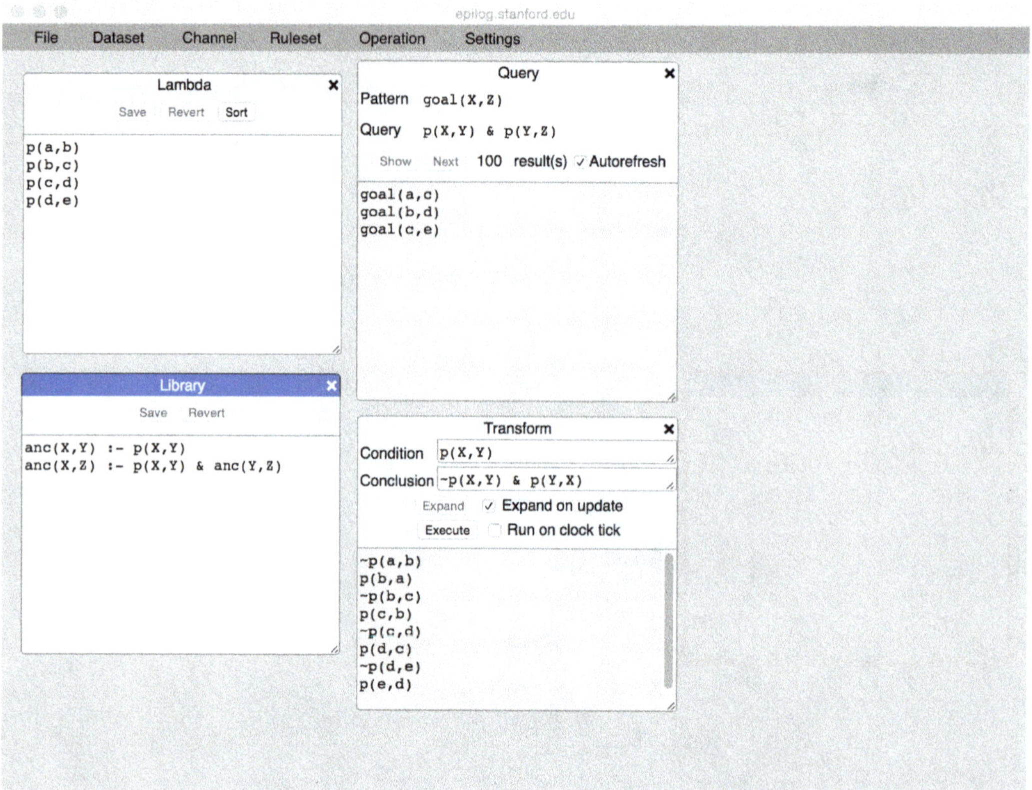

Once we have a view defined, we can use it in queries and transforms. We could, for example, open another query window and write a query using anc. However, there is a streamlined tool for this purpose, viz. Compute. Here we have clicked the Compute button and gotten an empty Compute window.

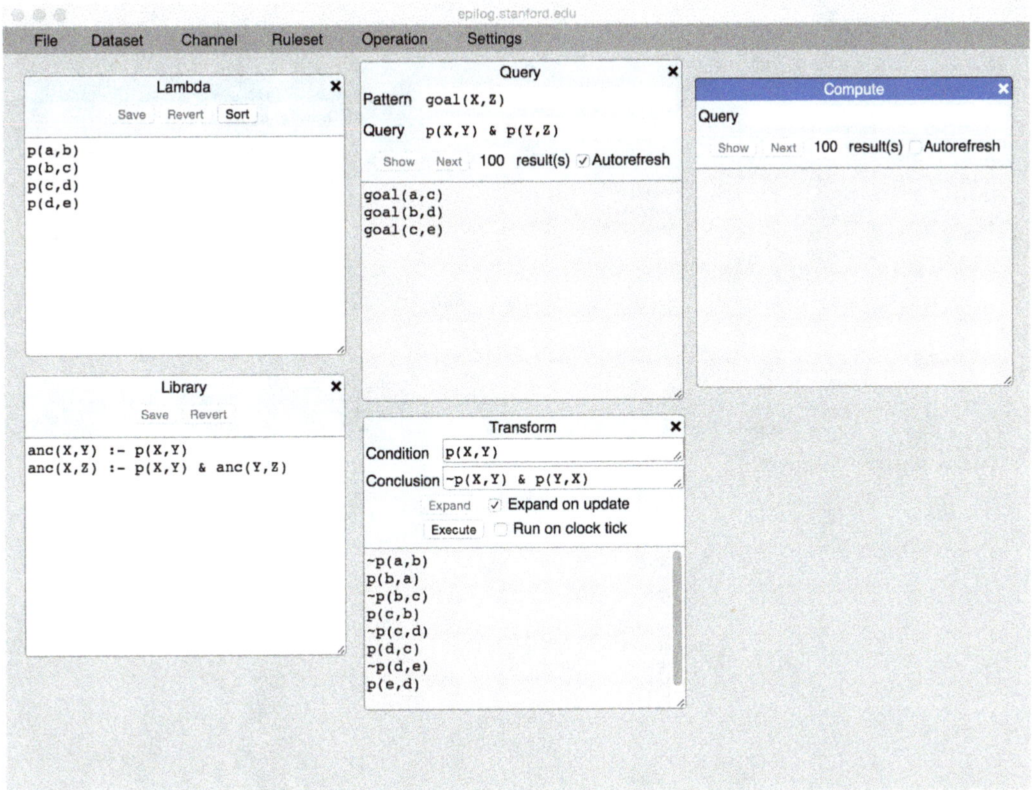

If we enter anc(b,Y) in the query field and press Show, we get a list of all facts in which b appears as the first argument.

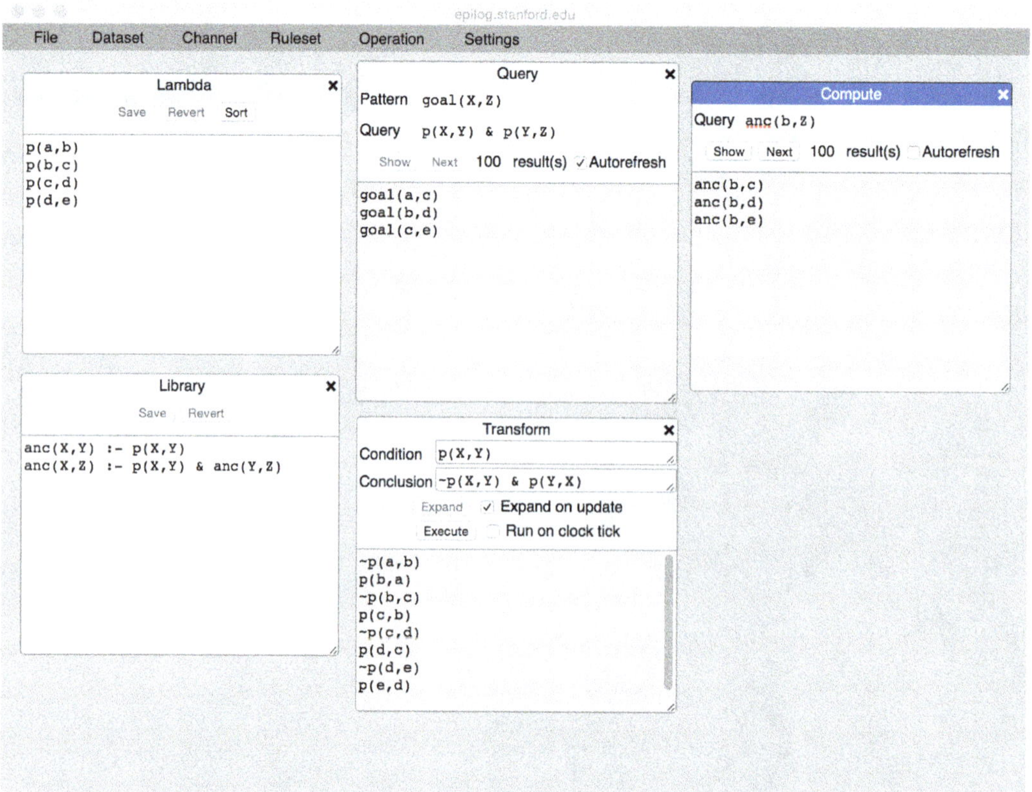

As with queries, if we check the Autorefresh box, Sierra will keep the display up to date as we make changes. For example, if we were to add an additional fact to lambda, the answer set would be updated as shown here. (Note that the Query and Transform windows have also been updated.)

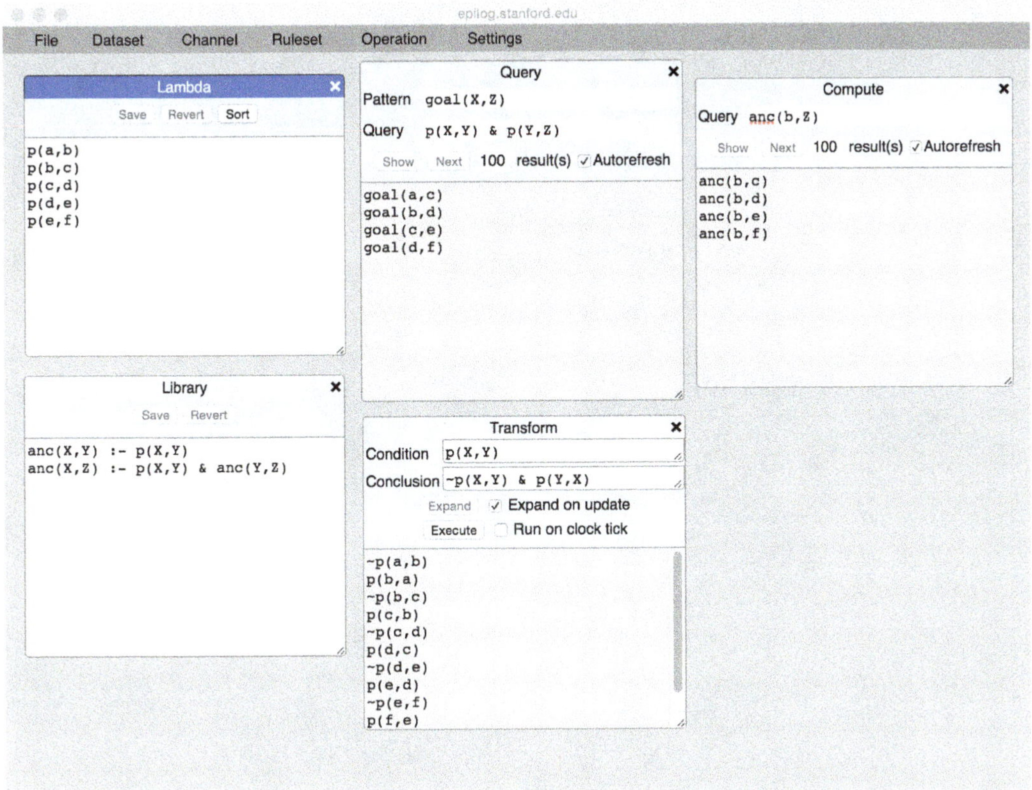

As with queries, it is possible to request a specific number of answers to be shown and to step through them using the Next button.

B.7 OPERATION DEFINITIONS

Operations in Logic Programming are effectively named transformations. As with views, an important benefit of this is composition. Once we have a named operation, we can use that name in defining other operations. Moreover, we can use the name in defining the operation itself, i.e., in defining recursive operations.

Operation definitions are expressed by adding rules to a ruleset, in this case library. Here, for example, we have defined the operation `purge`. On executing `purge(X)`, Sierra eliminates all children of p, all children of children, and so forth.

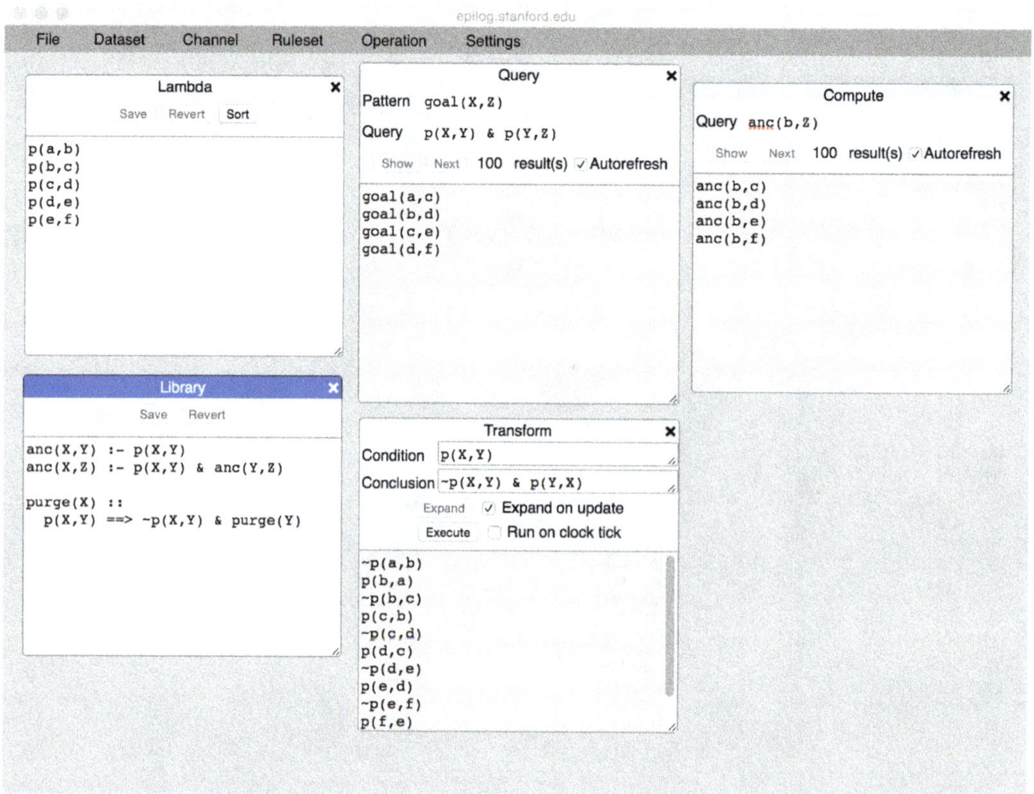

Once we have an operation defined, we can use it in transforms. We could, for example, open another transform window and write purge as a conclusion. However, once again, there is a streamlined tool for this purpose, viz. Execute. Here we have clicked Execute on the Tool menu and gotten an empty Execute window.

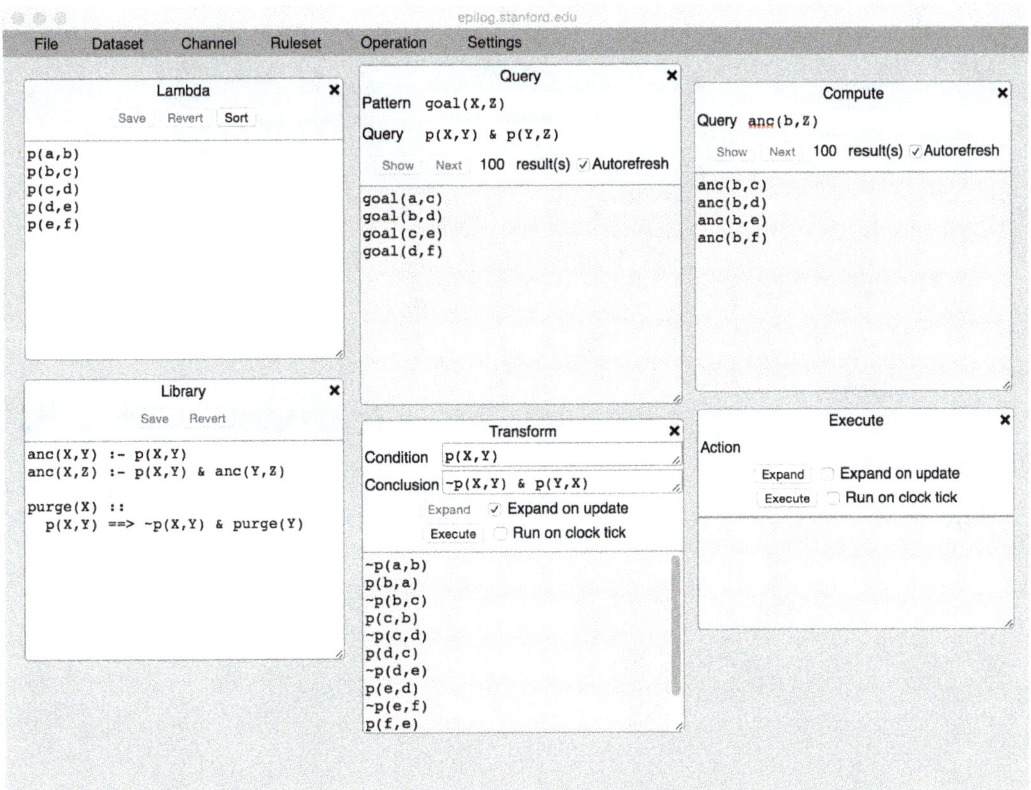

If we enter purge(c) in the query field and press Expand, we see a list of all facts that will be deleted if we execute purge(c). Note that, if executed, these facts would be removed in a single step, i.e., operation execution is an "atomic" action.

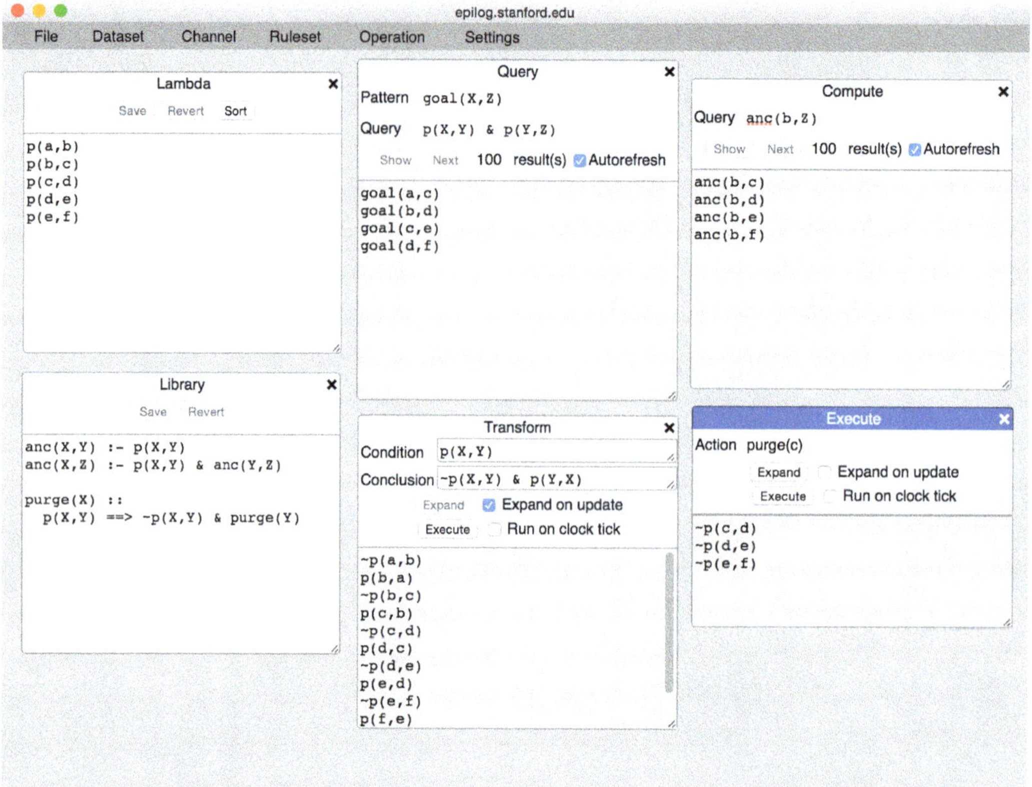

As with the Transform tool, we have the option of expansion on update and the option of running on clock tick.

If, at this point, we press the Execute button, Sierra will delete the indicated facts and update all windows accordingly, as shown here.

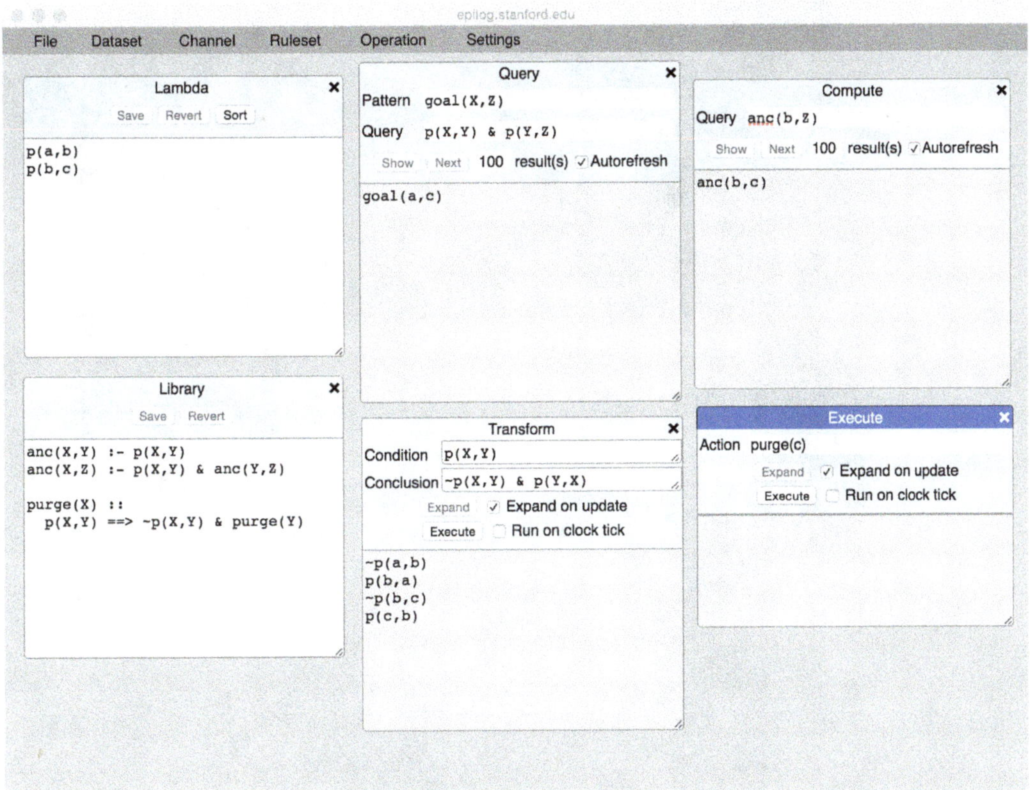

Although not illustrated by this example, operation definitions are extremely useful as event handlers for interactive user interfaces, e.g., browser-based worksheets.

B.8 SETTINGS

The Settings menu allows us to control the inference engine inside Sierra.

Clicking Queries brings up an interaction pane that allows us to specify the number of inference steps performed on an individual query before the system terminates its efforts.

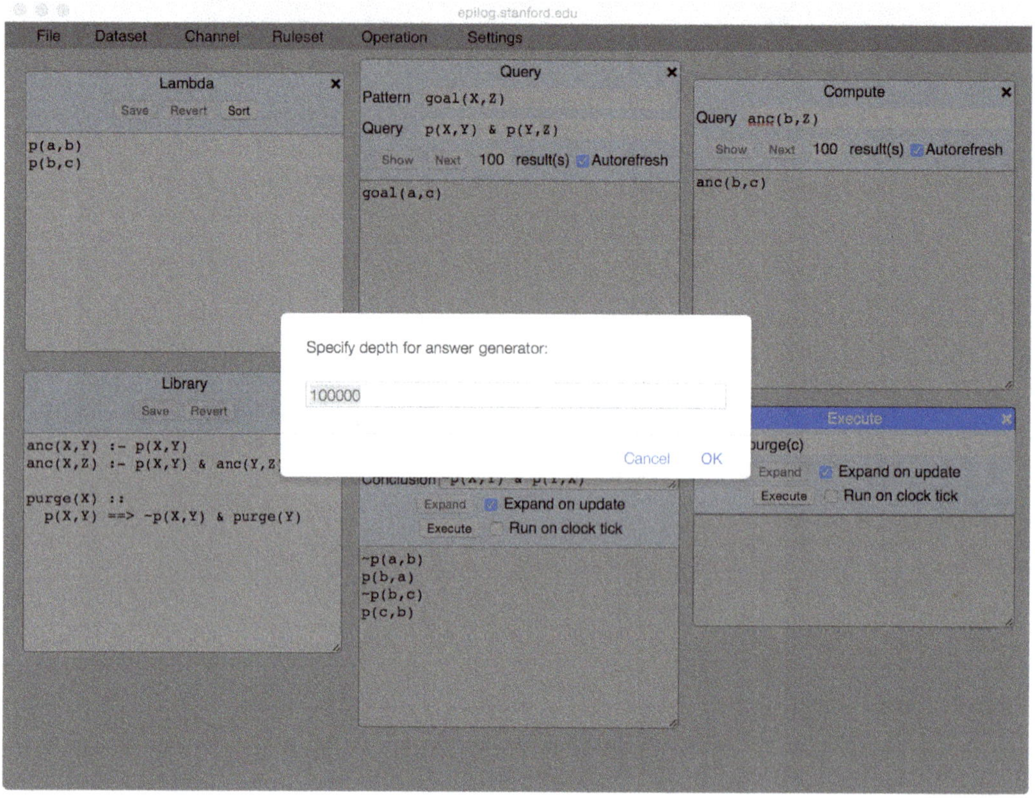

Clicking Transitions brings up an interaction pane that allows us to specify the number of depth of recursion in expanding operation definitions.

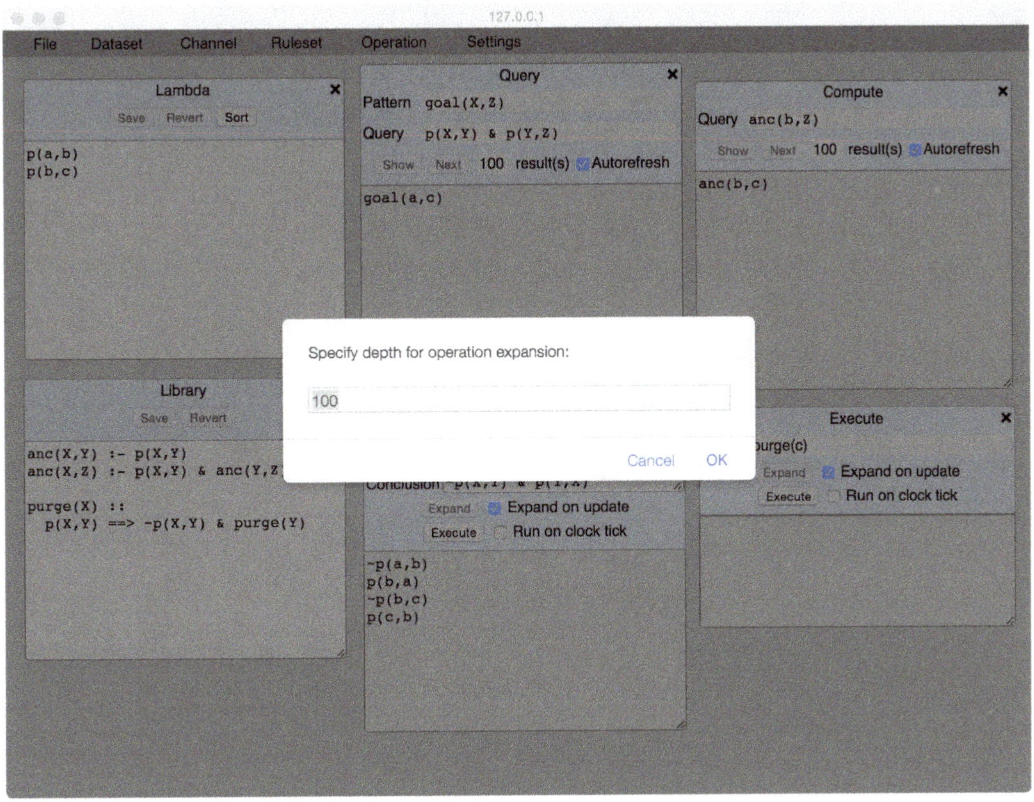

Clicking Timer brings up a window that allows us to set the timer going. This will run the operations in Transform and Execution windows where we have checked Run on Clock Tick.

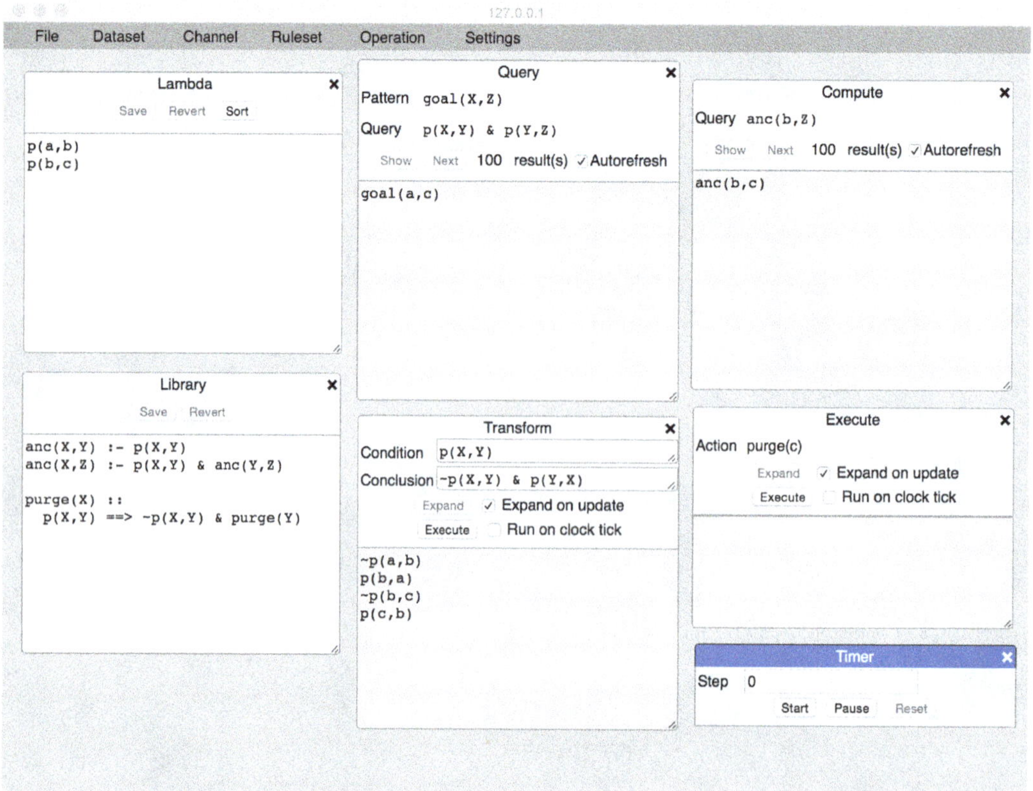

B.9 FILE MANAGEMENT

The Load option on the File menu allow us to read datasets and rulesets from the local file system and load them into library, lambda, or named datasets. The Save options allows us to write data from any window to the local file system.

The Save Configuration option allows us to save the complete state of Sierra to the local file system, including data, rules, settings, open windows, and so forth. The Load configuration option allows us to load a previously saved configuration file. These operations are extremely useful in developing Logic Programming applications. We can stop work and continue right where we left off on another day. And we can exchange demonstrations by sharing config files with others.

B.10 CONCLUSION

In addition to the capabilities described here, Sierra provides tools for manipulating communication channels, which allow flow of information between Sierra and external data sources and that enable collaboration between different incarnations of Sierra running on the same machine or other machines. Unfortunately, the details are a limited complicated, and so we have skipped over the details of these capabilities in this simple introduction.

Finally, it is worth noting that there is an extension of Sierra, known as Halle, which is intended for use in developing interactive, web-based worksheets. In addition to the capabilities described here, Halle provides tools for laying out these worksheets in WYSIYG fashion, displaying those worksheets as separate windows in a single Sierra-like web page, and interacting with those worksheets while allowing authors to view and edit the underlying data and rules in Sierra-like fashion.

Comments and complaints to `genesereth@stanford.edu`.

References

[1] C. Baral and M. Gelfond, Logic programming and knowledge representation, *Journal of Logic Programming*, pp. 19–20 and pp. 73–148, 1994. DOI: 10.1016/0743-1066(94)90025-6.

[2] A. J. Bonner and M. Kifer, Transaction logic programming, *Proc. of the 10th International Conference on Logic Programming*, Budapest, Hungary, 1993.

[3] V. K. Chaudhri, S. J. Heymans, M. Wessel, and S. C. Tran, Object-oriented knowledge bases in logic programming, *Technical Communication of International Conference in Logic Programming*, 2013.

[4] K. L. Clark and S.-A. Tarnlund, *Logic Programming*, Academic Press, 1982.

[5] W. F. Clocksin and C. S. Mellish, *Programming in Prolog*, Springer-Verlag, 1984. DOI: 10.1007/978-3-642-97596-7.

[6] C. J. Date, *WHAT Not HOW—The Business Rules Approach to Application Development*, Addison-Wesley, 2000.

[7] R. Dechter and D. Cohen, *Constraint Processing*, Morgan Kaufmann, 2003. DOI: 10.1016/B978-1-55860-890-0.X5000-2.

[8] D. DeGrout and G. Lindstrom (Eds.), *Logic Programming: Functions, Relations, and Equations*, Prentice Hall, 1986.

[9] M. Gelfond and Y. Kahl, *Knowledge Representation, Reasoning, and the Design of Intelligent Agents: The Answer-Set Programming Approach*, 1st ed., Cambridge University Press, March 10, 2014. DOI: 10.1017/cbo9781139342124.

[10] M. R. Genesereth and M. L. Ginsberg, Logic programming, *CACM*, 28(9):933–941, 1985. `http://dl.acm.org/citation.cfm?id=4287` DOI: 10.1145/4284.4287.

[11] M. R. Genesereth and A. Mohaptra, A practical algorithm for reformulation of deductive databases, *SAC*, Limassol, Cyprus, 2019.

[12] C. Hewitt, Planner: A language for proving theorems in robots, *IJCAI*, 1969.

[13] P. Hayes, Computation and deduction, in *Proc. of the 2nd MFCS Symposium*, pp. 105–118, Czechoslovak Academy of Sciences, 1973.

[14] R. Kowalski, Predicate logic as a programming language, in *Proc. IFIP Congress*, pp. 569–574, Stockholm, North Holland, 1974.

[15] R. Kowalski, Algorithm = logic + control. *CACM*, 22(7):424–436, 1979. DOI: 10.1145/359131.359136.

[16] R. Kowalski, *Logic for Problem Solving*, North-Holland, 1979. DOI: 10.1145/1005937.1005947.

[17] R. Kowalski, The early years of logic programming, *CACM*, 31:38–43, 1987. DOI: 10.1145/35043.35046.

[18] R. Kowalski and F. Sadri, Programming in logic without logic programming, *TPLP*, 16:269–295, 2016. http://www.doc.ic.ac.uk/rak/papers/KELPS DOI: 10.1017/s1471068416000041.

[19] V. Lifschitz, *Answer Set Programming*, 1st ed., Springer-Verlag, October 3rd, 2019. DOI: 10.1007/978-3-030-24658-7.

[20] J. W. Lloyd, *Foundations of Logic Programming*, Springer-Verlag, 1988. DOI: 10.1007/978-3-642-83189-8.

[21] S. H. Muggleton, *Latest Advances in Inductive Logic Programming*, Imperial College Press, 2015. DOI: 10.1142/p954.

[22] M.-L. Mugnier and M. Thomazo, An introduction to ontology-based query answering with existential rules, *Proc. of Reasoning Web: Reasoning on the Web in the Big Data Era*, 10th International Summer School, Athens, Greece, September 8–13, 2014. DOI: 10.1007/978-3-319-10587-1_6.

[23] F. Rossi, P. Van Beek, and T. Walsh (Eds.), *Handbook of Constraint Programming*, Elsevier, 2006.

[24] L. Tekle, Subsumptive tabling beats magic sets, *SIGMOD*, 2011. http://logicprogramming.stanford.edu/readings/tekle.pdf

[25] J. McCarthy, Programs with common sense, *Symposium on Mechanization of Thought Processes*, National Physical Laboratory, Teddington, England, 1958. http://www-formal.stanford.edu/jmc/mcc59.ps

[26] J. McCarthy, Generality in artificial intelligence, *CACM*, December 1987. DOI: 10.1145/1283920.1283926.

[27] J. Minker, On indefinite databases and the closed world assumption, in *International Conference on Automated Deduction*, pp. 292–308, Springer, Berlin, Heidelberg, 1982. DOI: 10.1007/bfb0000066.

[28] S. J. Russell and P. Norvig, *Artificial Intelligence: A Modern Approach*, Pearson Education Limited, 2016.

[29] M. J. Sergot, F. Sadri, R. Kowalski, F. Kriwaczek, P. Hammond, and H. T. Cory, The British Nationality Act as a logic program, *CACM*, 29(5):370–386, 1986. `http://complaw.stanford.edu/complaw/readings/british_nationality.pdf` DOI: 10.1145/5689.5920.

[30] J. D. Ullman, Bottom-up beats top-down for Datalog, *PODS*, 1989. `http://logicprogramming.stanford.edu/readings/ullman.pdf` DOI: 10.1145/73721.73736.

[31] J. D. Ullman, *Principles of Database and Knowledge-Base Systems—Volume II: The New Technologies*, Computer Science Press, 1989.

Authors' Biographies

MICHAEL GENESERETH

Michael Genesereth is a professor in the Computer Science Department at Stanford University and a professor by courtesy in the Stanford Law School. He received his Sc.B. in Physics from M.I.T. and his Ph.D. in Applied Mathematics from Harvard University. Genesereth is most known for his work on Computational Logic and applications of that work in Enterprise Management, Computational Law, and General Game Playing. He is one of the founders of Teknowledge, CommerceNet, Mergent Systems, and Symbium. Genesereth is the current director of the Logic Group at Stanford and co-founder and research director of CodeX (the Stanford Center for Legal Informatics).

VINAY K. CHAUDHRI

Vinay K. Chaudhri is formerly a program director in the Artificial Intelligence Center at SRI International, and currently affiliated with the Stanford Computer Science Department. He received his Ph.D. in Computer Science from University of Toronto, Canada. Dr. Chaudhri is a recognized expert on artificial intelligence, including knowledge representation and reasoning, question answering, ontologies, and knowledge acquisition. At Stanford his activities include promoting logic education for secondary schools, investigating techniques for rapidly acquiring formal knowledge and productizing intelligent textbooks. He consults with the financial industry on computable contracts and knowledge graphs. He has also taught courses on knowledge representation and reasoning and logic programming.

CPSIA information can be obtained
at www.ICGtesting.com
Printed in the USA
LVHW060421011020
667371LV00004B/153

9 781681 737225